Praise for the Authors and *Accelerate*

"I have seen Walter, a Hall of Fame speaker and his coauthor/wife of three decades perform in many different venues, from several Jersey Mike's National Conferences to the standing-room-only hotel conference centers. I always had a front row seat! Their message changes to connect to the audience; from store managers/district managers to multi-unit, multi-concept owners to C-suite professionals. And every time, without fail, the crowd reacts with an applause so authentic because the message was well received, and the message was REAL.

Walter's earlier book *Swim!* taught us leadership and our responsibility to mentor. Their next co-authored book, *Cultivate*, taught us leadership and the 6 nonnegotiable traits of a winning team.

It's important to understand their history to understand their new book, *Accelerate*. Walter and Antoinette create a power couple, and through their love comes their guidance at every level. Through their life experiences—including the NBA, raising a family, and Hall of Fame speaking engagements with the Canadian franchise association, as well as meeting industry leaders—the Bond family brings their A game.

Success is never fast without direction. It takes a plan. Inside these pages, you will find a straightforward approach that can take a business owner to the next level or any leadership team that may need a new play to create more directional goals.

Their coaching experience through the decades will be obvious and well worth the time invested. It will help you and your team to better communicate with great intention. After all, isn't this the reason why we all do what we do? To teach, mentor, and grow our systems? You can't do this alone. You need a team like the Bonds for guidance and, most of all, validation to your approach. With that said, dedicate time to analyze, organize, strategize, prioritize, and systemize—as the Bond family coaches us—UP!

They are simply coaching you from afar. Enjoy their approach as I have personally done for over 10 years."

—Mike Manzo, COO and 40-Year Employee, Jersey Mike's Subs

"As a former *Inc. Magazine* Entrepreneur of the Year and founder of three successful companies, I wish *Accelerate* had been available to me when I started my entrepreneurial journey. The path to success would have been a lot less bumpy."

—Michael Block, former CEO, Block Business Group Inc.

"*Accelerate* offers a compelling, research-driven framework for understanding how organizational practices can drive high performance. Walter has spoken at many of my franchise conferences and consistently delivered the right information tailored perfectly for our audience. I have no doubt this book will be as informative, energetic, and inspirational as his presentations, offering practical insights that any growth-focused leader can apply."
—Jason Parker, Cofounder and Co-CEO, K9 Resorts

"*Accelerate* is a great book for entrepreneurs. Walter and Antoinette blend strategic insight for the accelerated growth of an enterprise and encourage the reader to dream big. It sparks a sense of purpose and possibility."
—Bill and Beverly Parker, Philanthropists

"Walter and Antoinette have been both trusted clients and invaluable mentors to me. As any business owner knows, building something meaningful comes with constant challenges, shifting market conditions, and moments of doubt. Without a coach or mentor, that journey can often feel isolating. Their guidance has not only helped me navigate difficult decisions but has also illuminated paths I never could have found on my own.

Their mentorship has been a true gift—offering clarity, confidence, and solutions when I needed them most. One of the greatest lessons they've imparted is that true acceleration often requires the wisdom to slow down. That principle has become a cornerstone in our firm's growth strategy.

To this day, I continue to learn from their unwavering dedication, insight, and generosity. I'm endlessly grateful for their impact and the continued inspiration they bring."
—Jaque Bethke, Chief Visionary Officer, JAQUE

"Walter and Antoinette are two of the most dynamic and gifted speakers I've ever seen. They are right up there with Tony Robbins in engagement and enthusiasm but have a more approachable delivery."
—Jason Anderson, President, Vast Coworking

"I've known Walter and Antoinette for years. The passion, wisdom, and commitment that fueled Walter in his professional career as an NBA player together with the knowledge and wisdom Antoinette adds is a must-read for anyone who wants to jump-start their business success."
—Mickey Rosenzweig, CEO, Rosenzweig Financial Services

ACCELERATE

Also by Walter Bond

Swim!

How a Shark, a Suckerfish, and a Parasite Teach You Leadership, Mentoring, and Next Level Success

A modern leadership parable that explores the powerful lessons of mentorship, teamwork, and success through the engaging story of unlikely ocean companions.

Cultivate

The Six Non-Negotiable Traits of a Winning Team

An essential guide for leaders and team members who want to build a culture of excellence, trust, and accountability by mastering six foundational traits.

All Buts Stink!

How to Live Your Best Life and Eliminate Excuses

A motivational blueprint for taking ownership of your life, cutting through the excuses, and unlocking your true potential.

ACCELERATE

A Champion's Playbook
to Fast-Track Your Business Success

WALTER AND ANTOINETTE BOND

Matt Holt Books
An Imprint of BenBella Books, Inc.
Dallas, TX

Accelerate copyright © 2026 by Peak Performers Huddle

Matt Holt is an imprint of BenBella Books, Inc.
BenBella Books, Inc.
8080 N. Central Expressway
Suite 1700
Dallas, TX 75206
benbellabooks.com
Send feedback to feedback@benbellabooks.com

Matt Holt and *BenBella* are federally registered trademarks.

Printed in the United States of America
10 9 8 7 6 5 4 3 2 1

Library of Congress Control Number: 2025044592
ISBN 9781637748503 (hardcover)
ISBN 9781637748510 (electronic)

Editing by Lydia Choi
Copyediting by Kaya Skovdatter
Proofreading by Jenny Bridges and Lisa Story
Text design and composition by PerfecType, Nashville, TN
Cover design by Brigid Pearson
Printed by Versa Press

Special discounts for bulk sales are available. Please contact bulkorders@benbellabooks.com.

To the families who bet on each other—
and decided that building something meaningful
together was worth everything.

To the spouses who turned their love into legacy.
To the siblings who became business partners.
To the parents who said, "Let's do this,"
and the children who grew up watching grit,
sacrifice, and bold belief in action.

This is for the family partnerships that are often unseen,
but whose fingerprints are on every breakthrough,
every pivot, and every triumph.

You are the living proof that business isn't
just about products or profits—
it's about people who choose to rise, together.

This book is a tribute to your commitment,
your unspoken code of loyalty,
your relentless drive to turn shared vision into generational victory.

***Accelerate** is your anthem.*
It's for the moments when quitting would have been easier,
but unity and belief kept you building.

You are not just growing a business—
you're cultivating a blueprint for what's possible
when family becomes the foundation for greatness.

To every family forging a future—
This is your time. This is your movement. Now, Accelerate.

CONTENTS

FOREWORD

In a world that constantly demands more, many of us find ourselves caught in the relentless cycle of activity—working harder, pushing further—yet still feeling unfulfilled and uncertain about our next move. Beneath the surface, there's a longing not just to succeed, but to live with purpose, clarity, and impact.

Accelerate is the invitation we've been waiting for.

Walter and Antoinette Bond don't just speak from success—they lead from experience. Their story is one of resilience, vision, and divine alignment. They've faced the setbacks, the stalled seasons, the uphill battles of entrepreneurship—from launching franchises to building their own training company. And through it all, they've uncovered a set of powerful, time-tested principles that transcend industry, season, and background.

This book is more than a collection of good ideas. It's a playbook for breakthrough. A system that cuts through the noise and equips you to build a life of excellence and impact. Whether you're in business, leading a team, launching a dream, or simply longing for clarity, *Accelerate* offers a pathway to help you align the dream for your life with God's plan for your life—to help you move at the speed of your divine purpose.

When you align your efforts with God's way, you tap into unstoppable momentum. You'll discover what happens when you *write the vision and make it clear* (Habakkuk 2:2) and *walk in agreement with truth* (Amos 3:3). You'll be challenged to release control and embrace the strength that comes from faith over fear, discipline over chaos, and clarity over confusion.

So if you're tired of spinning your wheels . . . if you're ready to move from hustle to harmony, from scattered efforts to sustained momentum, from wishful thinking to purposeful building—this book is your next step.

Walter and Antoinette are the guides you want for this journey. Their insight will challenge you. Their story will inspire you. And their wisdom will accelerate you. It's time to stop winging it—and start building the life and legacy you were designed for.

Dr. J. Todd Mullins
Christ Fellowship Church

OUR STORY
From Setback to Setup:
Why We Built *Accelerate*

We didn't start as business experts. We started as believers.

Our very first business venture was a franchise. Coming from successful careers—Antoinette in sales and Walter as a professional athlete in the NBA and throughout Europe and South America—we believed we had what it took. Confidence? We had that in abundance. But experience taught us something far more important: **We didn't know what we didn't know.**

Very quickly, we found ourselves in the fire: working long hours, juggling bills, trying to keep up. We weren't just running a business . . . the business was running us. Eventually, it all came crashing down. To get out of a burdensome lease, our landlord required us to file for bankruptcy. That painful chapter became the end of our first business, but the beginning of our transformation.

So what went wrong?

We lacked foundational tools. We didn't understand how to build a strong team, create consistent customer traffic, or truly read the marketplace. And maybe most critically, we weren't passionate about the industry; we were chasing money, not meaning. And that's a losing formula.

Then came business number two.

This time, we had passion. We had drive. But when it came time to scale, we realized something vital: If your business foundation isn't anchored properly, growth doesn't create stability, it creates strain.

That's when we created the Accelerate Business Model.

It's everything we wish we had during those early years. A toolkit to think smarter, plan better, and grow with intention. Anchored by our signature **One-Page Plan**, annual audits, and a simple yet powerful strategy framework, Accelerate was built to help small business owners do more than survive. We want you to **thrive**, and not just in business, but in mindset, systems, team leadership, and long-term impact.

Today, we coach, train, and equip passionate entrepreneurs with tools we've tested, refined, and used ourselves. Our failures became the fire that forged our mission. And now, we're here to pass the torch to you.

To every small business owner out there pushing forward, building something meaningful, and daring to dream: We see you.

Cheers to your journey. Cheers to your acceleration.

—*Walter & Antoinette Bond*

NOTE TO THE READER

We wrote this book because we've been where you are: stuck, frustrated, and wondering what it really takes to break through to the next level. Early in our business careers, we knew we needed help ourselves, and through that process, we discovered something game changing: the value of a simplified, actionable business plan. Not just a plan that sits on a shelf collecting dust, but one designed to be put into practice now.

One of the biggest lessons we learned was the power of a ninety-day execution plan. It's not enough to have big ideas or lofty goals. The real magic happens when you break those goals down into manageable steps and focus on consistent, intentional action over time.

We also realized that *operations are everything* when it comes to scaling a business. You can't grow without systems and processes that are clear, repeatable, and easy to implement. Until you create a framework that anyone on your team can follow, you'll stay stuck in the cycle of doing everything yourself, and your business will never reach its full potential.

This book is the result of our journey from frustration to clarity, from hustling without traction to building a business that finally had momentum. We're sharing what worked for us so that you can avoid some of the pitfalls we encountered and *accelerate* your own growth.

Our goal is for Anthony and Ricki to serve as a mirror—for you to see parts of yourself in them. We hope you read this book and see a couple at a crossroads, two individuals who are willing to do whatever it takes to catapult their business to the next level. We hope that you see their drive, their commitment, and their passion and that it reignites something in you.

We also hope that you can see their weaknesses and realize that those same struggles might exist within you too. Whether it's battling self-doubt, perfectionism, fear of failure, or impulsiveness, Ricki and Anthony's journey is a reflection of the real challenges that come with chasing big dreams. Our goal isn't just to tell their story—it's to remind you that growth isn't linear, that setbacks are part of the process, and that success often requires looking inward as much as pushing forward.

If you simply read this book cover to cover, you'll have read a great story with relatable characters and walk away with valuable business fundamentals that will change the way you approach your business. But if you treat this book like an interactive experience, a living, breathing, working resource, your business will be transformed on every level.

When you see a QR code, stop, scan it, and answer the questions or do the activity on the website. Take the time to read about Anthony and Ricki's journey and then take the next step and apply it to your business *in real time*. That is what is going to make this more than just a story; this is the part that allows you to take action and start making changes *now*. Not when you finish the book, not in a week or two—*now*.

We know you have a choice when it comes to the information you choose to help *accelerate* your business, and we're excited to be a part of your journey. This book is designed to remind you that real progress happens when you focus on progress, not perfection. And it starts right here, right now.

Let's get to work!

CHAPTER 1

THE CRASHERS' CONUNDRUM
When Survival Isn't Enough

Anthony sank his muscular frame into the driver's seat, closed the door, and took a deep breath. The health club parking lot was deserted, lit only by a single flickering light in the center. His whole body was sore, exhausted from work and exercise. His intense workouts were the only thing that kept him sane, but he couldn't bring himself to put the car in reverse and head home just yet. It was too much. When Ricki had left the office at five, Anthony could tell something was wrong. Again. She did that thing where she made eye contact and said goodbye to everyone else in the office except him. She didn't say, "See ya at home," or ask him what he wanted for dinner—she just left. And right before she left, she'd sent him an email. *An email*, Anthony had thought. *That's how we communicate these days? Through email?*

He'd opened it up. It was only four sentences:

> The sales numbers this month are worse than last quarter. How are we supposed to pay the bills?
>
> Mrs. Cooper said she's going to shop around for a new shop for her fleet. She said something about us being unreliable.

That was it. He'd rested his hands on the top of his head and leaned back in his chair. It felt like this was all they talked about lately: the way their business was falling apart and how little cracks in their foundation were now causing the whole thing to crumble.

He had robotically moved through the rest of the day until he'd watched her practically speed out of the parking lot and out of sight. He sighed, resigned to the idea that he'd have to deal with it later.

And now it *was* later. 10:46 PM, to be exact. He didn't want to go home and dance around that awkward silence for an hour before someone fell asleep or Ricki asked a pointed, loaded question that he never had the right answer to, one of those questions that he knew didn't really have answers but were merely a way for Ricki to vent her frustration. He didn't want to go around and around about what to do and who to call and how to fix this financial mess they were in. He also didn't want to admit that he couldn't rescue the day like Superman, or confess that he hadn't done the one thing she'd asked him to do (have the conversation with Jodie), or have her pull up the spreadsheet on her laptop and show him, again, how in the red they were. He knew. He knew all of it already and was tired of having the same conversation every week, going to bed angry, waking up in awkward silence, driving to the office in that same awkward silence, and then plastering on a fake smile and trying to get through the day with minimal nagging or passive aggression.

Failure in anything was foreign to Anthony and Ricki. They used to attack their day together, work out together, and stay balanced together, but now Ricki worked and worried all day. No outlet, no respite, little to no sleep, and on edge all day long. Their failing business had taken over their lives. They were both struggling mentally and emotionally, though only Ricki let it be known in private. Anthony tried his best to act strong, optimistic, and like somehow, some way, it would all work out, even though he had no clue how. This former power couple was experiencing a power outage of epic proportions and hanging on for dear life. If something didn't turn around quickly, they would go belly up financially.

Anthony's phone vibrated in the cup holder. "Still at the gym?" Ricki texted. He took another deep breath and started up his sports car, which he'd bought when things had been going much better. When his phone connected to the car's Bluetooth, his playlist started up again, and he turned up the volume on his custom sound system as he peeled out of the parking lot. He thought maybe the noise would drown out his thoughts of failure. Thoughts about how everything seemed to be unraveling. It wasn't just the financial strain, though that was a massive part of it. It was also the distance growing between him and Ricki, the feeling that they were becoming more like roommates managing a crisis than partners in life. He thought back to their last tearful argument, where Ricki had yelled: "We've cut costs, doubled down on marketing, and put in long hours, and *nothing* is working! What are we missing?" The arguments, the resentment, the finger pointing—they all crowded his mind as he navigated the empty streets, each red light giving him another chance to contemplate what awaited him at home. They'd promised to not let being business partners affect their marriage, but that was exactly what was happening.

He could picture Ricki at home, probably pacing the living room floor, alternating between anger, worry, and suspicion. Anthony felt a pang of guilt; he felt like he could contribute more, but didn't know what or how, and that he'd been avoiding things that he shouldn't have, and his friendly and extremely laid-back personality didn't help the situation either, according to Ricki. The customers loved him, but when it came to the actual work—well, *Charm doesn't get it done*, as Ricki would say.

During his career as a running back, Anthony had prided himself on handling the pressures of the game with ease. On the field he was known for his world-class speed, agility, and quick decision-making, but he was quickly learning that those skills weren't exactly carrying over into this part of his life. Earlier that day, Anthony had overheard Ricki on the phone with her sister, Penny. He hadn't meant to eavesdrop, but he couldn't pull himself away.

"It's like he can't shift out of his football mindset," she'd said quietly into the phone. "You know, running backs have to focus on individual plays, not necessarily the whole game strategy. They just have to focus on the one play in front of them and where they need to be. I feel like that's what he does. Short-term thinking. I feel like I'm the only one stepping back to look beyond our immediate problems."

He wished he had just walked away. It stung, knowing that was how she felt about him. But it also stung because, deep down, he knew she was probably right.

The conversation with Jodie was just one more thing he'd put off, hoping it would somehow resolve itself. Because as big and strong as Anthony was, he did not eat tough conversations for breakfast, lunch, *or* dinner. If he was being honest, he hated tough conversations and confrontations altogether and avoided them like the plague.

As an elite former athlete, Anthony loved to entertain clients and could hold court with anyone. He was most comfortable being the center of attention when things were great, but the presentation didn't always match the output. Anthony didn't know or fully understand what his gift in business truly was. It felt like he was always in transition. He usually loved to drive fast, but tonight headed home as slow as possible to avoid yet another drama-filled night with the love of his life. Because he had no answers. And as the man of the house, he felt like he should.

As he turned into their neighborhood, his chest tightened. The familiar sights of home felt unwelcoming tonight. The house was dark except for the dim porch light. He pulled into the garage and sat a moment, hands gripping the steering wheel, and actually prayed that Ricki was asleep so he could make it through the rest of the night in peace.

He got out of the car and looked around the garage. It was a stark contrast to the rest of the house, which was meticulously clean, organized, and aesthetically pleasing. That was Ricki's domain. Out here was his space, a clutter of half-started projects: A lawn mower sat in pieces in one corner of the garage, and Anthony flashed back to last summer, when he'd decided he was going to start repairing all of their lawn tools instead of taking them to the shop down the street. There were picture frames that he swore he was going to sand and polish, and a halfway constructed birdhouse on his barely used workbench, a reminder of the time when he thought woodworking was going to be his new passion. Each project was a reminder of something he thought was going to be his new identity after football, each neglected and unfinished.

With another deep breath, he shut the garage door, closing it behind him. He rehearsed the apology he knew he'd have to give for his two-hour lifting session if Ricki was awake. His workouts were the only thing that allowed him to escape the reality of life and feel powerful like he had when he played in the NFL. Anthony had a decent pro career, but he really wanted to go back to the time when he was the big man on campus. Everyone had loved Anthony, and it would be great to feel like that again. He'd thrived all his life in sports, and everyone, especially Anthony, assumed he would do the same in business.

"Ricki," he whispered to himself, practicing. "I'm sorry. I know we're in a rough spot, and I know it feels overwhelming. This wasn't the plan, and I know I can do more." The words felt inadequate, but it was all he had. Anthony could charm his way out of almost any situation with his million-dollar smile and charismatic personality. But Ricki was done with the charm. And charisma alone couldn't pay the bills or meet payroll, and Ricki was not a fan or a groupie he could mesmerize. Ricki was a straight shooter and was not afraid to call Anthony on his BS.

As he opened the door quietly and stepped inside, he was prepared for just about anything, and the creak of the floorboards announced his arrival. The living room light flicked on, and there she was, standing in the doorway with tired eyes and crossed arms.

"Anthony," she began, voice soft but firm, "we need to talk."

||||||||||||

Anthony settled into his chair at the kitchen table and took a deep breath. *Here we go,* he thought. Ricki grabbed him a bottle of alkaline water and set it in front of him. He glanced up at the framed picture of the New York City skyline above the refrigerator and was instantly transported back to their honeymoon. How electric and alive their life had felt back then. They only had each other and felt like they could take on anything after football finally ended. They chose New York because it was the last city he'd played in, a big, bustling city full of possibilities, full of the kind of adventure they yearned for.

He remembered how they'd laughed over dollar slices of pizza and late-night Coca-Colas from hole-in-the-wall restaurants and held hands while wandering through Central Park, dreaming about the life they were going to build after his sports career was over. Back then, they'd believed that love and ambition were all they needed to face whatever came their way. But now? Now the weight of reality had settled on their shoulders like a heavy, wet blanket. The bills, the mortgage, the mounting pressures that never seemed to ease up. No more big NFL checks, and all of their NFL savings were invested in the business. Anthony knew Ricki, the gorgeous, beautiful control freak that he married, blamed him for that, whether consciously or subconsciously. As an all-star athlete, he'd always been able to make a big play to secure victory, but now he felt helpless.

Ricki had waited patiently for him to fulfill his football dreams, and the plan was for them to leverage her business skills and background with his brand and persona to build a legacy. Except the plan was not working.

She'd seen him do it on the football field year after year. Anthony was known as "Touchdown Tony," and had a knack for making the big play at the perfect time, leading his team to victory. The only time he'd failed in football was losing in the high school state championship to a small-town team that, as Anthony always added when he told the story, they "had no reason to lose to." It was the largest upset in Georgia high school football history.

Ricki knew they needed to talk, and they needed to find a way out of this. But for the first time, Anthony wasn't sure if they could. This once strong, unbreakable couple was falling apart, and it was all because of a failing business.

"Remember the honeymoon?" Anthony asked quietly, his voice barely above a whisper. Ricki looked up from where she was absentmindedly drawing circles with her finger on the kitchen table, her intense expression softening just a bit. Anthony had amazing social skills and knew how to diffuse situations like a bomb expert.

"Yeah," she replied, a hint of a smile tugging at the corner of her lips. "I remember."

"We were so sure we had everything figured out back then," Anthony continued, shaking his head. "But now . . ." His voice trailed off. They were like fire and ice, peanut butter and jelly, salt and pepper. Anthony was the ultimate people person; Ricki could take them or leave them. Ricki was a fierce competitor; Anthony was a performer and the ultimate showman—and together they were an unbeatable and unbreakable combination. Until now.

They sat in silence for a bit as Ricki cooled enough to let tonight not become another intense moment. They were good at this. After ten years of marriage, they'd learned how to be okay in the stillness, to not feel like they had to fill every moment with a word or a thought. He loved that they could drive long distances and have deep, meaningful conversations, but could also be perfectly content just being in the same space, enjoying the quiet.

"I was talking to Penny," Ricki said, finally breaking the silence. Out of habit, Anthony rolled his eyes, and the energy shifted quickly. Penny was Ricki's older sister, the one who always had something to say about their business, their marriage, their finances, and she was not a huge fan of Anthony's outsized personality or history as a smooth ladies' man. This always bothered Anthony, because while he *was* friendly, he had been fiercely faithful ever since Ricki became his girl. On their wedding day, Penny had pulled Anthony aside and said, "You better take good care of her. She is all the family I have left"—as if he hadn't spent the last few years proving he would.

Ever since then, Penny had made it her mission to offer unsolicited advice, always assuming she knew best. Anthony had never quite warmed up to her, because he'd already tried everything in his power to win over Penny. He wasn't Penny's number one fan, but for Ricki's sake he tolerated her and understood their family dynamics. When Penny was around, Anthony would almost shut down because the two of them together brought even more intensity out of Ricki. Penny had no interest in being charmed by Touchdown Tony, and she had this deep-rooted idea that football players just were not that smart. Ricki probably could have done better, according to Penny.

"What did she have to say this time?" Anthony asked, trying to keep his tone neutral, though he already felt the familiar tension creeping in. He didn't know what Penny had suggested, but he was already against it, simply because it came from her.

"She suggested we get away for a little bit. Take some time, go somewhere else, and use that time to really think, plan, recalibrate. We can't keep doing the same ol' thing and expect a different result," she explained.

Anthony started to interject, to let her know this was a crazy idea, that they couldn't just up and leave the business like that, but she put one finger up to stop him.

"Why not? I know you're worried about leaving the office, especially with things as they are," she continued. Anthony crossed his arms, annoyed at how well she knew him, but reminded himself that she became his wife because he respected her and her intellect.

"But Jodie and Antwon and Chris know what they're doing," Ricki went on. "They can manage without us for a little bit. They have 'manager' in their titles for a reason, babe. They can look after what we've built. We need to lead and build something better. And what good does it do to be there when we don't have a clear plan to turn this thing around? We're not doing anything transformational. We are at a clear crossroads in our business, and we need to do something different, and it seems like we are focused on surviving, but not thriving."

She paused for a second, giving him time to absorb what she was saying. "Babe, we can't keep doing this. Payroll is getting harder and harder to meet, and numbers are down at all locations. We knew the grim data of how few small businesses make it when we started—we just never thought we would become a statistic."

She stopped, and Anthony could tell she was thinking carefully about how to word her next thought.

"And Pen even offered to—"

"No," Anthony said firmly, cutting her off before she could finish. "We're not having Penny involved in this. I appreciate what she's trying to do, but this is between us, Ricki. I don't want her swooping in and trying to be a hero, like she always does. Why do you tell her all of our business anyway? She needs to mind her own business—that's why she can't keep a man. She has no boundaries. She trespasses constantly." Anthony stood up and started pacing the kitchen. Ricki was well aware of the rift between her beloved older sister and her husband and had played referee since day one. Penny was the only person on earth that could get under his skin.

Ricki took a deep breath and started again. "Penny did some interior design work for a couple who has a bed and breakfast on Martha's Vineyard. She said they owe her a favor, and she could get us a week there for next to nothing. It's quiet, isolated, and just what we need to get away from everything for a bit. We are athletes at the core, babe. Think of this as our off-season," Ricki said with a smile. She knew catering to the athletic side of him would soften him up a bit.

Any time Anthony was holding court with his friends and fans, he'd talk about how hard he would work in the off-season during his career. *The off-season is when you work on your business, and not in your business* was Anthony's favorite tagline.

Anthony took a deep breath, sat back down, and stared at the ceiling, thinking the idea over. A bed and breakfast sounded pretty good, but the fact that it was Penny's connection left a sour taste in his mouth. He didn't want to be indebted to her, even in a small way, or allow her to take any credit for their success. But the thought of escaping their reality and dreaming again was too much to pass up, even if Penny was involved. Being away from the constant stress of their lives felt like a lifeline where maybe they could breathe again and just hang out like they used to. And for Anthony, he knew that the off-season portion of his career was truly sacred for him.

"I don't know . . ." he said hesitantly. "It's not just Penny. What if we get up there and all we do is keep having the same arguments?

What if it doesn't help? We expect something magical just to happen because we're on the Vineyard? We do need a miracle, but just going as a change of scenery doesn't make much sense to me. In football, I knew exactly what I needed to work on in the off-season—it was no secret." He was reminded about the conversation he'd overheard between Penny and Ricki earlier but decided to let it go. "My off-seasons had a very detailed workout plan I followed."

Ricki leaned forward, her expression softening. "It's not about running away from our problems, Anthony. It's about giving ourselves a chance to breathe, to reset. We've been stuck in survival mode for so long that we don't even have the space to think straight. Maybe this is our chance to really figure things out, without the noise. No phones, no meetings—just us away from the rat race."

Anthony studied her face, seeing the mix of exhaustion and hope in her eyes. She wasn't angry, which meant Ricki had some hope coming back. She was right; they hadn't had a moment to catch their breath in months, maybe even years, since his career ended. *Life has been life-ing.* The constant grind was wearing them both down and affecting their marriage, and the walls they'd been building around themselves were only getting higher. They both knew they needed a business breakthrough but neither knew what to do.

He let out a long sigh. "Okay, why not?" he said slowly. "We'll go. But we do this our way. No Penny involved beyond making the reservation, okay?"

Ricki smiled, her eyes softening with relief. "Okay. Just us." She reached across the table and squeezed his hand. Anthony nodded, feeling a flicker of hope he hadn't felt in a while. He enjoyed seeing the same hope in his wife's beautiful face. Maybe getting away wouldn't fix everything, but it was a start. And right now, a fresh start was all they needed.

They sat in a moment of rare stillness. No accusations, no tension, just a quiet mutual understanding that something had to change.

Ricki leaned back in her chair, exhaled, and then said it.

"You know what I've been thinking about lately?" she asked, not waiting for a response. "Crashers."

Anthony raised an eyebrow.

"Remember what we used to call business owners who couldn't get out of their own way? The ones who were unprepared, reactive, always putting out fires but never really driving anything forward?"

Anthony nodded slowly. "Crashers. Yeah. The ones who were always a split second away from disaster."

"That's us, Anthony," she said gently. "We're Crashers right now. Hustling without clarity. Grinding with no GPS. Just hoping momentum alone will save us. But all we're doing is colliding with the same problems over and over."

The words hit harder than Anthony expected. But they weren't an accusation—they were a mirror.

"I don't want to be a Crasher," Ricki said. "I want us to lead again. To drive again. To be Accelerators."

Anthony gave her a long, steady look. "Then we'd better stop winging it and start steering."

Ricki smiled. "Exactly."

Sometimes when you're in a dark place you think you've been buried, but you've actually been planted.

—Christine Caine[1]

ACTION PLAN

Write a one-sentence vision for your business twelve months from now. Share it with a trusted peer or mentor this week. Schedule a thirty-day check-in on your calendar to review your progress toward this vision and adjust your strategy as needed.

CHAPTER 2

THE PIVOTAL PAUSE
Choosing Acceleration

The next morning, Ricki and Anthony walked into the office together. Crystal, their newest and youngest employee, was already at her place at the front desk, organizing papers and clicking away on the computer. When they walked through the door, she greeted them with a wide and genuine smile.

"Hey, guys!" she said cheerfully.

"Hey, Crystal," Anthony replied. "Do you have lunch plans today?" Crystal looked confused for a second, and shook her head.

"Great—then we'd love for you to join us for a team lunch meeting. We'll close up shop for about an hour and head over to Stu's BBQ."

"Yes!" replied Crystal excitedly. "I love that place. They have the best barbeque in all of New York, really good ribs, and the mac and cheese is delish."

Stu's BBQ was an iconic hole-in-the-wall spot that had been there for decades, known for its amazing food and equally amazing service. It made everybody happy.

"Excellent. Let's plan on wrapping things up here around 11:45, and then we can all head over together. I'll go tell the others," said Anthony.

Anthony and Ricki moved through the reception area and back into the heart of the office. As they passed each cubicle, they invited Antwon, Mary, Todd, Chris, Jodie, and Lewis to lunch. Ricki couldn't help but notice the way Jodie and Antwon looked a little hesitant before accepting the lunch offer. She wondered what they were thinking, and if they were worried that this was the conversation they'd all been dreading: that things just weren't going to get better and that everyone would need to start looking for a new job. It made her stomach hurt to think about having that conversation. These people had worked with them for so long and stood by them through everything. She knew they had families to support and financial goals they were working toward, and she couldn't stomach the idea of letting them down.

At 11:45, the office started buzzing with a different kind of energy. Ricki could hear the shuffle of papers being put away and office doors being closed. By noon, everyone was huddled around

Crystal at the reception desk, talking excitedly about the menu and what they were going to order, but Anthony could tell they were also a little nervous about what the meeting was really about.

Anthony and Ricki got into their car and pulled out of the parking lot, a parade of employee cars right behind them all trying to keep up with the fast-driving Anthony. They parked and waited for everyone else to arrive at Stu's. As the big sign on the hostess stand made clear: They wouldn't be seated until their entire party was present. Stu had a culture, and his regulars had been conditioned on how to act at his place. Like clockwork, the parking lot began filling up fast, though luckily they'd all made it right before the rush started.

The small, unassuming building sat in Brooklyn on a small piece of land that overlooked Manhattan, between a bait shop and a convenience store, its faded sign barely legible. The entrance door creaked as they stepped inside, welcoming them to a space that was a local hidden gem. No tourists could find it, and locals considered it a true Brooklyn natives' hangout. *If you know . . . you know.* Stu would smoke the meat all night and everyone raved about how it would fall off the bone. Some even described his homemade sauces as liquid sunshine.

The interior was dimly lit, with only a few booths lined up against the worn brick wall. Mismatched tables and chairs filled the middle of the room, each piece showing signs of age but holding its own kind of charm. In one corner, a few outdated arcade games blinked and hummed quietly, their screens casting a soft glow. The bar, built from weathered wood with a brass footrail, had seen years of elbows leaning, stories shared, and many lies told.

Behind it, shelves were stocked with every type of bourbon and house-made sauces in unlabeled bottles.

Stu, a Memphis native, had a simple business formula: Serve delicious food, provide great service, and create a place people liked to be. He had also done a wonderful job conditioning his customers on what they called Stu's Way. Everyone knew that they'd better get there early to avoid missing out on the goodies that day. His kitchen cooked up the day's portion, and once it was gone, it was gone. Stu put so much pride into the process of each dish: He refused to take shortcuts or whip up anything quickly, and his portions were generous—always plenty of leftovers to take home and enjoy for days to come. Everyone loved Stu, and Stu loved everyone. There was a rumor that Stu's BBQ was going to be on *Diners, Drive-ins and Dives*, one of Ricki's favorite shows. This secret Brooklyn paradise was almost on the verge of stardom, yet Stu had never bought an ad and didn't know the first thing about social media. Many Wall Street guys and private equity executives from Manhattan would complain about how Stu ran his business, but he never budged. "You run Wall Street, but this is my street," Stu would tell them with a chuckle, but he meant every word he said.

Southern blues music played from a vintage jukebox near the bar, its tunes weaving through the air, blending with the clatter of dishes and laughter from nearby tables. Ricki glanced around, taking in the eclectic decorations, old license plates, faded photos of local BBQ competitions, and a hand-painted mural depicting a smoky pit with a pig donning a chef's hat. Instinctively, her eyes went to a framed picture behind the bar. In it was her late father, Richard, shaking hands with Stu, back when Stu had a lot more hair and a lot less beer gut. Stu had been one of Richard's closest friends—they'd met through mutual friends when they both lived in Memphis, and although she didn't know exactly how, Ricki knew that her dad had played a role in keeping the restaurant from closing decades earlier.

She'd always meant to ask Stu about it, to hear the story of how and why the two connected and the part her dad played in keeping the doors open. The few times they'd tried to talk about her dad, it was either bad timing or Stu would get so emotional he could never get the words out. But there *was* a back story there—she just didn't know all the details.

She always knew her father was a successful businessman. It was one of the things she admired most about him. It was his inspiration that kept her up late studying, and why she had always pushed herself to be the best in everything she did. Richard might not have been book smart, but he was an amazing businessman.

Ricki remembered how much her dad cared about people, and how he had a way of seeing potential in people and places that others missed. It was that quiet drive, that deep belief in others, that had shaped the person she had become. Her dad loved to plan, and had an unwavering commitment to doing things the right way even if it took more time. She had such fond memories of sitting with him at his desk, as he carefully arranged his neatly labeled folders to line up perfectly with the edge of his desk. She missed the way he would just randomly offer words of wisdom. He'd say, "Ricki, a solid foundation might not be glamorous, but it's what keeps the walls standing when the storms hit," or "It's not about the sale you make today, it's about the customer who comes back tomorrow because you built something worth their loyalty." As a high schooler, she wasn't always quite sure what these little nuggets of wisdom meant, but she loved the way his face lit up when he said them.

Looking back, Ricki realized that her dad had an uncanny ability to make running a business look effortless—but now, as she was struggling to run her own, she knew better. She wondered if he'd felt the same pressure she was feeling, and if he had, how he was able to do it without it showing. Every time they lost a client or she received another past due notice in the mail, she heard a small nagging whisper that told her she wasn't measuring up. She constantly worried whether she was good enough to fill his shoes, and, if she let herself get really honest and vulnerable, she knew it was why she felt the need to obsess over every detail and do everything herself. She didn't just want her business to succeed—she *needed* it. She needed the validation that she could do what her father had done. If she could just get this business to soar, maybe it would finally quiet that nagging voice that told her she wasn't enough.

Ricki shook herself from the memory of her dad and turned her gaze toward a string of Christmas lights that hung year-round over the bar, blinking out of rhythm but somehow fitting perfectly with the mismatched charm of the place. Something about Stu's BBQ made you feel at home, that you could forget your life's issues.

As they waited for the rest of their group to squeeze into the remaining booths and tables, Anthony nodded to the pitmaster behind the counter, a burly man in a grease-streaked apron, an avid football fan who knew all about "Touchdown Tony" and his football prowess. He gave a quick wave before returning to the smokers. The atmosphere buzzed with the sounds of sizzling meat, smoking wood, scraping chairs, and the soulful strains of blues, making Stu's BBQ feel like the heart of the town's best-kept secrets. If you closed your eyes, it felt like you had been teleported to Memphis. The culture of Stu's BBQ was unique and beloved, and it had been created over decades. After one visit to Stu's, you were better prepared for the next one. There was no place like it in all of New York or its surrounding boroughs.

Once they were all seated and had ordered their drinks, Anthony, the company's spokesman, cleared his throat, and the table quieted. "I just wanted to thank you all for joining us for lunch today. I want to say up front: Don't be nervous. This meeting is not bad news. Things are not fine, but all of you still have jobs." Anthony let out a little laugh, and Ricki noticed how nobody laughed with him—instead, everyone let out a deep exhale, seeming relieved. They looked at Ricki for reassurance, because they knew Anthony was the face but Ricki was the heartbeat.

"It's no secret that things have been a little rough around the office lately," Anthony continued. "We're fully aware that the numbers aren't where we want them to be, our online reviews are not ideal, and production and efficiency have definitely slowed down over the last year or two. We are so grateful for all of you and the time you dedicate to this dream of ours of running a truly great auto shop. The struggles we're facing are not a reflection of you or your commitment to this company—they're more about our leadership and the direction my wife and I have provided. Business is tough, but we promise we will figure this out and right the ship. We *will* get this football across the goal line." Some people got what he meant, and some didn't. Anthony always used sports analogies; he couldn't help it.

"Ricki and I have had a lot of conversations lately, and we know that the problems in our business start right here." Anthony pointed to himself. "We started this business years ago with high hopes, big dreams, and a plan to change the industry. But over time, we've lost sight of that plan, and as a result it's been like the blind leading the blind. We can't expect you to fulfill orders, meet deadlines, and work toward goals if we don't even know what those deadlines and goals are. So we wanted to get everyone together today to let you know that Ricki and I will be heading out of town to do some recalibrating. We're going to take a week to clear our minds, sit down, and really talk about the future of this business and how we can get back on track. We're confident that all of you can hold down the fort while we're gone. We trust you and know you're equipped with everything you need to be successful, even when we're not around. And we have always appreciated your hard work and effort. This is not about hard work, this is about working smarter."

"I will say," Ricki added, "that's one thing we did really well. We've created a team of go-getters, hard workers, honest and loyal people who we know can get the work done even when we're not here. We're lucky to have you all. You've stuck by us through everything, and we're grateful to be able to go do this work knowing everything will be fine at home." Ricki looked around the table. Jodie, Sam, and Crystal nodded gently. Even though Anthony and Ricki fought behind the scenes like cats and dogs sometimes, they always had a united front at work in front of the team.

"So, where are you going?" asked Crystal.

"We're heading up to Martha's Vineyard," Anthony replied. "We'll be gone for a week, and when we come back, we'll be recalibrated with a new plan. That's the goal: to go up there and clear our minds, rethink everything, and really examine every aspect of this business to see what we should be doing better or differently. Ricki and I met as college athletes, and for athletes, an off-season is sacred. It is when you work *on* your business and not *in* your business. When we get back, we'd love to have another meeting to debrief and share our thoughts with you and work together to create a new vision for this business moving forward."

Ricki squeezed Anthony's leg under the table. She was proud of him for his honesty, vulnerability, and humility.

Slowly, the conversation around the table shifted to the menu. Anthony looked over at Ricki with a small smile. She returned it, and although he didn't know what the next few days had in store for them, he was thankful to be facing it with her by his side.

When the bill came, Ricki started digging in her purse for her wallet and getting worked up about which card actually had enough room on it. Ricki was not only part owner, she was part juggler of all their accounts payable and receivable. But Anthony's ego sometimes got the best of him, especially when a crowd was present.

"Uh, uh," Anthony said quietly. "Don't even think about it—I got it."

He fished his corporate credit card out of his wallet and laid it face up on top of the bill. Ricki shook her head and sighed nervously to herself. *I hope it goes through,* she thought. They both had the same card; the money came from their shared business account. But for public optics, he was so insistent on being the one to put the card down. Years earlier she had tried to explain that it didn't matter whose card they used, but Anthony didn't want to hear any of it. He had mumbled something about how the man should pay or how it was his responsibility as a provider, and at the time she just hadn't wanted to argue. They were already arguing about enough at that point—she didn't need another fight over who was going to put a credit card down to pay for a meal.

Ricki conceded, put her credit card back in her purse, and chatted quietly with the team until the waiter returned with his card and asked for a signature. If that card came back declined, Anthony would have been mortified. Clueless the card was almost maxed, he gave a huge tip as he signed the check, and Ricki said a silent "hallelujah." She knew they'd dodged a bullet and saved her husband's precious ego from embarrassment. Things were that tight.

After lunch, the team headed back to the office. Ricki sat down at the computer and checked her email, noticing a message from Penny:

> *Hey Ricki—*
>
> *Everything is good to go with the reservation. Stanley and Edna are excited to see you and have reserved the Tulip Room for you (expertly designed by yours truly). I've attached their contact information in case you need to get ahold of them. They*

were able to bring the total rate down to $500, and I took care of it for you. (Don't tell big TDT.)

Love you, sis. I'm glad you're doing this. Let me know if you need anything. And remember, every-one calls Stanley "Coach"!

—P

Ricki closed out her email and stood up, preparing for her final walk-through of the office before she left for the day. She picked up her trusty clipboard, and when she looked up, one of the managers, Brandon, was standing in the doorway.

"Oh hey. Didn't see you there. What's up?" Ricki asked with a smile. She took a quick inventory of his body language and noticed that he seemed a little nervous. He stepped into her office and shut the door. *Uh oh,* Ricki thought.

"Hey, boss. Listen, I was thinking about what you said at lunch today, and I've been meaning to talk to you. Do you have a second?" Ricki gestured at the chair on one side of her desk and sat back down in hers.

"Okay, I'm just going to be up front here," said Brandon. "I was going to hand in my two weeks' notice this week."

Ricki's eyes widened.

"I know I haven't been here that long, but there have just been a few things that I've noticed that make it hard for me to do my job. I wasn't going to bring it up, but after the conversation at lunch today, I figured I should at least give you a chance to hear some of the issues. Wouldn't be fair if I just left and didn't give you a chance to hear where I'm coming from and maybe make some changes."

Ricki could tell he was being as gentle as he could, and she appreciated him being thoughtful in his responses.

Brandon went on. "Like for instance, the organization. I feel like each week when I come in, the parts are in a different place or we have a different system for how things get sorted. I feel like I spend a lot of time looking for parts, and I'm not even sure if we have them or where they are."

Ricki nodded as he continued.

"And Hector does his best, but I feel like there is no clear method for us to track what needs to be done versus what has been done. And sometimes things that are low priority get put in front of things that are high priority. I have dealt with a few angry customers the last few weeks, and it just makes it so that I'm not excited to come in to work." Ricki noticed the pained expression on his face.

"But I like you guys, and I like the team, and I don't want to quit," said Brandon. "So I figured I'd just let you know about some of these things. I didn't want to just leave without giving you a chance to address them."

Ricki's stomach churned, but she kept the smile on her face. She stood up and held her hand out to shake Brandon's.

"I really appreciate your honesty, and I'm sorry that things have felt disorganized here for a while," she said. "That's what Anthony and I are trying to fix. Will you hang on this week until we're back?"

Brandon thought for a second and nodded. Ricki exhaled and followed him out of the office so she could get back to her last-minute walk-through of the office—though now she had a lot more on her mind.

Her first mission was to swing by Carla's station near the service counter. She leaned against the counter and waited for Carla to get off the phone, while noticing a scattering of parts receipts that weren't stacked neatly on her desk. Ricki had to stop herself from organizing them.

"Did you get a chance to call the parts distributor and let them know about the new schedule?" Ricki asked once Carla got off the phone, trying to sound casual.

A quick movement of Carla's eyebrows told Ricki she was confused, but she quickly recovered. Ricki knew Carla was good at her job—Ricki had just been telling Anthony that she was one of the best new hires they'd had in years.

"Yes, I did it yesterday," Carla replied with a patient smile. "They've confirmed, and the delivery is on track."

"And you got written confirmation?" Ricki asked.

Carla nodded, but when Ricki didn't move on, she added, "I'll double-check." She quickly clicked through her emails until she found the confirmation and showed it to Ricki.

Once Ricki saw the confirmation, she gave a tight smile and moved on. She trusted Carla, but she couldn't stop thinking about all the things that could go wrong if something was missed. It wasn't that her team didn't know what to do, it was that Ricki just couldn't stop herself from catastrophizing.

Her next stop was the garage, where she found Hector in his oil-stained overalls running a diagnostics test on a minivan. She spotted a clipboard with Hector's notes for the day sitting on the workbench. She walked toward the bench to pick it up and read it, but Hector got to it first.

"Hey, boss," Hector greeted her as she approached. "Everything's good. I ran through the checklist for the tune-ups, and all the fluids are topped off. Parts came in yesterday, so we're all set for the afternoon repairs."

Ricki glanced at the clipboard he was holding, skimming his detailed notes but trying not to look obvious. She knew Hector was meticulous—it was one of the reasons she'd hired him on the spot when he interviewed three years ago—but now she had Brandon's conversation replaying over and over in her head. Hector had been a mechanic for over a decade before he came to work for Accelerate Auto Repair, and he didn't need her micromanaging. Still, Ricki found herself glancing toward the car and back at the clipboard, double-checking for any oversights. Hector's smile faltered a little bit when, instead of walking away, Ricki stood there for another few minutes and then started walking around the van. Out of the corner of her eye, she could see that he'd raised an eyebrow, but she was thankful he didn't say anything. Ricki knew he was a little bit irritated with her, but she ignored it. By this point, Hector knew it wasn't personal; he knew she just needed to see for herself.

Her final stop was back in her office, where she pulled up the accounts payable report. The overdue invoices stared back at her like a silent accusation. She didn't have time to dig through every line item, but she couldn't stop herself from analyzing the numbers one more time. Maybe there was a solution she hadn't seen yet. *When was the last time Anthony even looked at this?* she thought to herself. *Not everyone can just avoid it like he does. If I don't fix it, it won't get fixed. If and when we get more money, I can fix it. We need more money.*

Ricki glanced at the clock, her heart racing as she realized that it was almost time to go. Anthony would come waltzing in here any minute without a care in the world about everything that could go wrong while they were gone. Her eyes moved to her father's worn brown leather recliner that sat in the corner of her office, faded spots where he used to rest his elbows on the arm rests. As a little girl, Ricki used sit in her daddy's lap in that same recliner after soccer practice. And while the chair didn't match the office decor, Ricki just couldn't bring herself to throw it away. By keeping it, she could remember her dad's spirit—the way the recliner squeaked when he kicked the footrest down, and the way it always smelled like cigars and his cologne. She glanced at the empty chair and could almost hear his deep laugh and him saying, "The pursuit of perfection is a roadblock to progress," when she'd storm into his office after a hard day at school or on the soccer field.

Nobody had been in that seat for eight years now, and she was thankful that Anthony had never even suggested that they move it. She liked having it there; it was a good reminder of who he was and who she wanted to be.

There are risks and costs to action. But they are far less than the long-range risks of comfortable inaction.

—John F. Kennedy[2]

ACTION PLAN

Identify one major decision or change you've been avoiding in your business. Write down the decision and the reasons you've hesitated. List the risks of staying the same versus the potential benefits of making the change. Commit to taking the first concrete step toward this decision within the next seven days—then schedule a follow-up date to review your progress and adjust as needed.

CHAPTER 3

THE OFF-SEASON BEGINS
Preparing for Strategic Growth

Anthony appeared in the doorway of Ricki's office and knocked lightly on the door frame. "Are you ready to get out of here? We should go now if we want to swing by the other locations before we go. And we want to beat traffic—you know I hate traffic," Anthony said, an excited smile on his face.

Ricki quickly closed her laptop, picked up her purse, and followed him out. They said a quick goodbye to the team, answered some last-minute questions, and reassured them that they'd be back with a new plan and a new vision.

Ricki settled into the passenger seat. (Anthony always insisted on driving.) The streetlights blurred past as Anthony's voice filled the car, listing every landmark he wanted to visit in Martha's Vineyard: the Gay Head Cliffs, the gingerbread cottages in Oak Bluffs, the Edgartown Lighthouse. He veered into his thoughts about comparing the charm of staying at a B&B to the privacy of a hotel, words pouring out in a steady, relentless stream. Ricki glanced at the buildings outside, worried about what she maybe forgot to do back at work. Anthony's nervous energy hummed between them, words tripping over each other like waves on the shore. *What was he anxious about?* She pressed her fingers against her temples, trying to find a moment of silence, knowing she forgot to do *something*, trying to sift through her own tangled emotions. But his chatter pulled her back, every sentence snapping at the edges of her focus and scattering her thoughts.

They pulled into their second location on Garrison Avenue and put the car in park. Right away, Ricki noticed the trash cans outside were overflowing and that Bernardo was leaning against the wall by the front door having a cigarette *and* scrolling on his phone. When he looked up and saw them approaching, he quickly put his phone away and stood up straight.

"Hey, boss!" he said too enthusiastically. Ricki gave him a disapproving glance. He knew the rules about cell phone use and smoking, but apparently Dave, this store's manager, wasn't enforcing them. She made a mental note to talk to him about that. They had opened this second location about three years ago and had spent a lot of time and energy training their employees so that this location would run exactly like their flagship store. But as Anthony held the door open for her and she walked inside, she could see things were slipping. The waiting area was disorganized, and the girl at the front desk was also on her phone. Ricki stood there for a moment waiting for Tina, according to her nametag, to notice they were there.

"Oh hi, hey. Hello. How can I help you?" she said flatly. She clearly didn't know who Ricki and Anthony were. Just then, Dave came rushing out from his office.

"Anthony! Ricki! Hey there. Didn't know you were coming in today," he said, coming out from behind the counter to shake their hands.

"We're heading out of town for a week, but we wanted to check on the other stores before we did," Ricki said, looking around. "And I guess it's good that we did. Can we go into your office for a second?" she asked, moving that way before Dave had a chance to respond.

Once they were all settled, Anthony spoke.

"Business is a little slow at this location, wouldn't you say?"

"Slower than last year, yeah. But we still have busy days," Dave replied.

"And that girl out there? Trina?"

"Tina," Dave corrected.

"Isn't she your third new hire for the front desk in the last few months?" Anthony asked. Ricki was surprised he knew.

"Uh, yeah. Marci quit, and then Shannon stopped showing up," Dave said sheepishly.

Ricki was kicking herself for letting things get this far. This location was a mess, the team was clearly not working together, and based on the empty garage bays, nobody was coming in.

"What about some of those marketing strategies we discussed last quarter? Did you see any of those bring in new business?" Anthony prodded.

"Uh, yeah, a little," Dave stammered. Ricki knew he had no idea what Anthony was talking about. Ricki saw Anthony's muscles tense and his grip strengthen on the arm rest.

"Okay. Well, we are going away for a while to come up with a new plan, a new vision. And when we get back, we will have everyone together to discuss how we want to move forward," said Anthony.

"And *who* is going to move forward with us," Ricki said, glaring across the desk at Dave.

After they said their goodbyes to Dave, Ricki introduced herself to Tina and reminded her of their "no cell phone use except on breaks" policy, then followed Anthony out to the parking lot.

"That was a mess," Anthony said, and Ricki could hear the anger in his voice. She nodded.

"I don't even want to go to Fillmore," he groaned, looking at her in a way that she knew meant he was hoping she'd agree and they could skip visiting their third location.

"We have to," she sighed.

On the way over, Ricki filled Anthony in on the conversation she'd had with Brandon. Anthony was as surprised as she had been, and she could tell that his feedback stung. "Well, that's why we're doing this, right? To fix it," Anthony said resolutely.

When they arrived, Ricki was happy to see the storefront was clean and organized, there were cars in the parking lot and in the garage bays, and friendly uniformed employees were helping customers with their car repair needs. Ricki and Anthony looked at each other hopefully as they walked into the store.

"Ricki! Anthony! Good to see you!" Yolanda, the general manager, greeted them. They followed her back to her office and sat down. "What brings you in?" she asked with a friendly smile.

They explained that they were going away and what their plan was for their return, and Yolanda listened carefully. But as Ricki took note of Yolanda's body language, she couldn't help but feel that something was off.

"How are things running here, Yolanda?" Ricki asked, trying to keep her tone casual.

"Great! Numbers are good, getting more repeat customers. Lots of good reviews," she added with a smile, but Ricki could tell she was nervous.

"Anything else we should know about?" Ricki pressed.

"Um, not . . . no, not really. Nothing we can't handle," Yolanda replied.

"*Nothing*? We're not pointing fingers or trying to get anyone in trouble. We just want to make sure you're okay," Ricki said gently.

Yolanda was quiet for a minute and then said, "I mean, you know how it is. Sometimes big personalities can cause drama in a small space like this. But we're handling it." She looked away and organized the already organized pile of papers on her desk. Anthony caught on to her hesitation and looked over at Ricki, who shrugged.

"Yolanda. What is it? You can tell us. We're here to help you. You're one of the main reasons this location has been successful. We're on your team," Anthony said.

"Okay, well, if we're being honest," said Yolanda, "there's been some drama, some tension, among some of the managers here. Seems like they all have a different vision for how the store should run, and they're butting heads a bit." She looked up at them and continued. "It's not like they're fighting, but it's snide remarks and offhanded comments here and there. High school stuff, eye rolling, gossip, not covering for each other. And then it's like the employees feel like they have to pick sides, which is starting to pit them against each other too. I'm worried the customers are going to start to feel the tension." She let out a deep breath.

Ricki asked if she had spoken to each of them individually and Yolanda said she had, but that everyone was being kind of vague with their answers, not wanting to get in trouble. They discussed the idea of planning a team-building retreat to bring everyone together, and Anthony promised to help her rebuild team morale when he got back. "Can you hang in there until we get back?" Anthony asked. Yolanda nodded and smiled and thanked them for their help, and promised she'd call them with any issues.

Back in the car, Anthony and Ricki were silent.

"How do all of the managers have a different vision of how things should be done? We taught them all the same things. We trained them just like we trained the other stores," Anthony said, his voice rising.

"I know. I don't get it. I thought when we opened the new locations it would just be copy and paste of our first location."

Ricki sighed. If she was nervous to leave town before, it felt almost paralyzing now.

As if he could read her thoughts, Anthony put a hand on her leg and squeezed. "Going is the best thing we can do right now. We have to. They'll all be okay until we get back. And when we do we'll be able to walk right into all three stores with a clear vision. A path forward." He squeezed her leg again, put the car in reverse, and headed home.

She practically jumped out of the car as soon as Anthony put it in park in their driveway. She quickly moved up the front porch, into the living room, and right into their home office to check her email, even though she had been obsessively checking it on her phone the entire ride home.

It felt strange that they were really going to pack up and leave, especially when things at work had been so unpredictable. But she kept coming back to the truth: This was what they needed, and they weren't going to be able to make it in this business if they didn't do something different. She was almost shaking with nervous energy, paralyzed by the idea of relinquishing control. She held a tinge of resentment for Anthony, who she felt was already checked out and had begun his off-season getaway prematurely.

Anthony made his way upstairs, and Ricki reluctantly followed. She was exhausted. It had been a stressful and emotional day at the office, and they still had packing to do. She also had to make reservations for the ferry that would take them to Oak Bluffs. She was usually so excited about traveling, but something about this trip was different. Not only was she worried about leaving the office at such a vulnerable time, but it felt like this trip came with a unique sense of pressure. This *had* to work. She'd tried everything to keep them from drowning, but it felt like they were just putting bandaids on problems. She forced herself to keep moving, to carefully move her clothes from the drawer into her packing cubes, creating a mental list of what to bring. She considered each item carefully before she packed it, debating what was right for a trip to Martha's Vineyard. On the other side of the room, Anthony was haphazardly tossing T-shirts, semi-folded jeans, and a few polo shirts into his bag.

There was so much she wanted to say, but she let it go. She knew her attention to detail drove Anthony crazy sometimes, especially when she tried to get him to do the same. But if things were going to get done right, it was her job to make them happen. Instead of saying any of that, she focused on her packing, smoothing out some of the wrinkles in her shirts. Her movements were steady, but her mind was racing.

"Are we going to the same place?" Anthony asked with a smile, pointing to her already bulging suitcase.

Ricki gave him a half smile and continued her methodical packing. But then she started to think about his comment. Was she overpacking? Was it the *right* things? *I'm overthinking this*, she thought, shaking the worry from her mind and moving around the room collecting the last of her things. Then she stopped, stalled out.

Anthony noticed and moved quickly across the room to her. He held her hand and said, "It's okay, babe. Everything will be fine while we're gone. You're not doing this alone. We're a team." He squeezed her hand. She looked up at him and smiled, but her stomach felt tight. She appreciated the words, but did he mean it? Did he really know what it felt like to juggle all of the small details of everything; the business, the trip, them? Did he ever feel like if he dropped the ball that all of it would spiral out of control?

"I know," she said finally. "I just don't want to mess this up. I don't want to mess *us* up."

Anthony moved in closer and wrapped his arms around her until he felt her relax. When he released her, he moved across the room and into their bathroom to shower. She sat at the edge of the bed and took a deep breath. Why was it that even though she put so much thought into all of it—the checklist at the office, the packing, the planning—she still felt like she was missing something important?

After her shower, Ricki joined Anthony on the couch downstairs. He had ordered Chinese and was setting it all out on the coffee table in front of the TV. Just as she settled in with her chopsticks, a buzzing sound came from Anthony's pocket. Anthony answered the phone with a big smile on his face.

"Hey, Mr. Chen! How are you, sir? How are the wife and kids? Did I just see on Facebook that you guys were in California?" Anthony listened carefully for a moment, nodding. "Sounds like a great trip. What can I do for you?"

More silence. Ricki tapped Anthony on the leg and cocked her head. *What's up?* she mouthed. Anthony put up one finger as he listened.

"Oh, yeah. Sure, Mr. Chen. We can handle that, no problem. I'll make sure that it's done by Monday. Only the best service for one of our favorite customers!" Anthony said, standing up from the couch and pacing the living room. Ricki felt like she was seeing him transform right in front of her eyes, turning on that charm and charisma that came so naturally for him. She tried to make eye contact with him as he paced, slightly worried about what he was promising.

"Yep, yep. I'll personally make sure it gets done. No worries." A beat of silence, and then: "Yes, sir. You too. Talk then." Anthony hung up the phone.

"What will be handled by Monday? Did you forget that we're going out of town? We're supposed to be taking a step away, not diving right back into the mess. What happened?" Ricki asked, all of her questions running together.

"Oh, it's fine. Mr. Chen loves me. He ordered a part for his truck and just needed me to check and see when it was supposed to be delivered."

"Okay," Ricki said slowly, "but we aren't going to be here."

"Ricki, he's cool. It's fine," Anthony said, gesturing with his hands to slow down. "I'll call the store on our drive tomorrow and have someone check on the shipment. And worst case scenario, I'll check on it when we get back."

"And what happens if we forget, or if something happens in the meantime? Did you let Crystal know? Did you let anyone know? Do you have any plans on looping anybody else in on this?"

Anthony sighed, his big smile fading fast. "I'll handle it," he said firmly.

"See, this is what you do. You rely on your charm and charisma to tell people what they want to hear, but then there's no follow-through. You love winning people over, you love being the good guy, you love saving the day. But then we don't have any systems in place for you to actually follow through with what you say you're going to do. And then things fall through the cracks."

"It's one client, babe. It's okay," Anthony said, trying to diffuse the situation.

"No, that's the thing," said Ricki. "It's not one client. It's *every* client. It's the way you work."

"It's called building relationships. You act like I'm just out here being buddy buddy with everybody for no reason. Building and maintaining relationships is what keeps the lights on and the bills paid. You act like it's not important."

"It is important, but so is the follow through. We won't be able to keep all of these relationships you spend so much time building if we can't deliver on what we promise," said Ricki.

They sat in silence for a while, and suddenly the Chinese food that had sounded so good earlier didn't look very appetizing to Ricki.

"Well, sorry for trying to keep people happy," Anthony said, stabbing his chopsticks into his container of lo mein.

There was so much more Ricki wanted to say, but she knew it was pointless. She pushed her food away, grabbed the remote, and changed the channel to a home remodeling show that she knew Anthony didn't like. As expected, he picked up his takeout and disappeared into the kitchen, leaving Ricki to watch her show in silence.

The next morning, Ricki woke up exhausted. She hadn't slept very well, but that was pretty typical these days. She'd tossed and turned thinking about Dave, Yolanda, and that clueless girl at the front desk on her phone. *What was her name? Tara?* She'd dozed off and then dreamed about angry customers showing up at her door or walking into work and realizing everyone had quit. After hitting snooze twice, she'd finally hauled herself out of bed.

She and Anthony moved through the house efficiently, finishing up their last-minute packing, picking up around the house, and checking emails. Ricki couldn't stop thinking about her conversation with Yolanda and was disappointed in herself for letting things get so bad at that store. She was replaying their conversation in her mind when Anthony appeared in their bedroom doorway.

"Ready to go?" he asked, both of their suitcases in hand.

She smiled at his chivalry and followed him, said goodbye to the dogs, sent a quick text to the neighbor to let her know they were leaving and that she could come over any time to pick the dogs up, grabbed a few bottles of water from the fridge, and headed out to the car while Anthony turned off all of the lights and locked up. As she got settled into her seat, she watched Anthony place all the luggage into the car. She couldn't help but notice the way his bulging arm muscles carried the cases like they didn't weigh a thing. And while life after sports had allowed him to develop the tiniest bit of a beer gut, Anthony still was looking good for his age. She could still see his strong athletic frame almost like it was when she met him in college. *He's still got it*, Ricki thought with a smile.

||||||||||||

Back in college when they met, Ricki was unstoppable—or at least that's how everyone described her. A star soccer player with impeccable grades, she seemed to have it all figured out. Her days were a blur of early morning practices, back-to-back classes, and evenings filled with studying or working her part-time job. She didn't have time for parties, let alone guys. The few who tried to get her attention quickly learned that Ricki wasn't interested in distractions or dumb frat guys. She had her eyes on bigger things, and she was so focused on soccer and school she was like a machine. Her plan was that as soon as school ended, she would launch a business just like her dad. Few guys had the courage to approach her, let alone ask her out. To this day, Ricki didn't fully understand how popular she'd been with the guys on campus. But she was a beautiful boss chick, and that was intimidating to some. Nobody would dare waste their time with a weak presentation, but Ricki didn't even notice. She always had laser-like focus and was a fierce competitor. If there was such a thing as too much focus, Ricki was guilty as charged.

Anthony was no stranger to focus and dedication either, but he loved a good time too. As a star running back on the college football team, he spent most of his time on the field or in the weight room. He thrived on competition and discipline, pouring every ounce of his energy into being the best. But even with all the intensity that came with being an athlete, Anthony was the life of every party, and women would throw themselves at him. Anthony had it all: brains, looks, and confidence. He was the full package, and he could literally have any girl he wanted on campus. But once he set his eyes on Ricki, that was it—he knew what he wanted.

He'd noticed Ricki long before she noticed him. Whether it was around the sports complex or passing her on campus, Anthony couldn't help but admire her drive, and he loved the fact that she wasn't into him. She was different from any other girl on campus: serious, determined, and entirely uninterested in attention. She was gorgeous, even though her hair was always in a ponytail and she never wore makeup or dressed up. Anthony loved all that, but it was the fire in her eyes that intrigued him most. He also loved that Ricki was not caught up in the college life or his campus persona. Anthony found that refreshing. He would sneak into soccer games with shades on and his college issued hoodie pulled over his head just to see her. Everyone assumed Anthony was a fan of the women's soccer team, but he was no soccer fan—just a Ricki fan. While everyone thought he loved soccer, he was actually falling in love with Ricki. And they had never even met. One more challenge for Anthony to conquer: to win over Ricki.

They crossed paths a few times. Once, he tried to talk to her in the library, leaning casually against the desk she'd claimed with a fortress of textbooks. He thought he was smooth, asking her something about a class they both had. She barely looked up.

"Sorry, I'm in the middle of something," she'd said, her tone polite but distant.

It wasn't a rejection exactly, but it was enough to let him know he'd need to try harder if he wanted to get her attention. And the fact that she was not caught up in his reputation or charm made him desire Ricki even more. In fact, she didn't know who Anthony was or his position in campus life.

Then the perfect opportunity came unexpectedly when Ricki got injured during a soccer game on a dirty play. A bad slide tackle left her with a sprained ankle and an excruciating recovery process that confined her to the training room. For someone as active as Ricki, it was torture. She spent her sessions with the athletic trainers quietly seething, her focus on healing as quickly as possible so she could return to action as soon as possible. She attacked rehab just as hard as the game.

Anthony saw the injury as it happened and had even thought about running onto the field like Romeo to check on his damsel in distress, but he stopped himself before he blew his cover. He knew athletic protocol: Ricki would be subject to the training room for recovery. Anthony hatched a plan to make his move through her treatment. He wasn't proud of it, but desperate times called for desperate measures. There is always a silver lining, and as a running back he was always looking for an opportunity to score a touchdown. He knew if he could win Ricki over, the girl he loved from day one, he would leave campus with a championship trophy wife.

The next day, Anthony strolled into the training room clutching his shoulder, wincing dramatically in pain. The tough stud running back who never missed a game all of a sudden had a serious injury to his shoulder. It confused his trainers, teammates, and all his coaches. When did Anthony get hurt?

"Banged it up during drills," he told the trainer, who arched an eyebrow but didn't question it further. Anthony wasn't just any player; he was the star of the team. If he said he needed treatment, no one was going to argue. He never missed a game or a practice, but if Ricki was getting treatment, so was Touchdown Tony.

He timed his sessions perfectly, making sure they overlapped with Ricki's rehab. The first few days, she barely acknowledged him, focused as ever on her own treatment and exercises. But Anthony wasn't one to give up.

"You too, huh?" he said one afternoon as he settled onto a bench near her.

She glanced at him, unimpressed. "Yeah. Ankle. You?"

"Shoulder," he said with an exaggerated sigh. "Can't catch a break this season."

"What do you play? Football?" she asked, unsure of the answer, her tone neutral.

"Running back," he confirmed, smiling. "And you're soccer?"

She nodded, and that was the end of the conversation. For now.

Over the next few weeks, Anthony found every excuse to come into the training room to talk to her and to get phantom treatment on his perfect shoulder. At first, their exchanges were short, just a few words here and there, but eventually, she started to warm up. They bonded over their love not just for winning, but for being champions. They swapped stories about their toughest games. Ricki and her team were national champions, and so was Anthony's team. He'd never admitted it to anyone else, but losing the state championship in high school still haunted him, and he eventually got around to sharing this deep, dark secret with Ricki. For the first time, Ricki felt like someone truly understood her drive and the pressure she put on herself. She loved how Anthony could make her laugh and take her mind off all she worried about—just like her dad could, minus the cigar. And Anthony loved how Ricki just got things done with no fanfare and no need for attention. They were different and the same all at once. They fit together like salt and pepper, peanut butter and jelly. Anthony was the happiest he'd ever been in his life—no other girl on campus mattered anymore. Ricki was everything he'd thought she was and more. Anthony, *however, had one issue: He was doing his best to hide the fact that his shoulder was perfectly fine.*

The first time Ricki finally laughed at one of his jokes felt like a victory greater than any touchdown he'd ever scored.

"You're funny, I'll give you that," she said one afternoon, shaking her head as he launched into another story about a disastrous team prank gone wrong.

"Glad you think so," he replied, grinning.

Her cheeks flushed, and she quickly turned back to her exercises.

As weeks turned into months, their connection deepened. By the time Ricki was cleared to play again, Anthony didn't need to fake an injury anymore; their friendship had expanded beyond the training room. They began to go to movies when time permitted and even went out on dates that had to be maneuvered around both of their busy schedules of school, practice, and games. He had won her trust, and her heart—but he had to figure out how to come clean with this little white lie he'd used to get close to her. In the meantime, word had spread very fast on campus that Anthony had landed Ricki as his girlfriend. This made him immortal. This dude was the man. There was nothing he couldn't do.

Years later, Anthony proposed on the fifty-yard line of their college stadium, where they had shared so many memories and both won national championships. She said yes without hesitation, tears of joy streaming down her face. But as they celebrated, he hesitated, pulling her close.

"There's something I need to tell you," he said, his voice low.

She froze. "What is it?"

"My shoulder," he confessed, rubbing the back of his neck sheepishly. "It was never injured."

Her jaw dropped, and she stared at him in disbelief. "What! You faked it?" she squealed, playfully slapping his chest.

"I had to," he said, smiling despite himself. "You weren't exactly easy to approach. I figured the training room was my best shot."

Ricki shook her head, torn between exasperation and laughter. "You're unbelievable."

"Worked, didn't it?" he said, holding up the ring on her finger.

She laughed, finally leaning into him. "I guess it did."

From then on, the story of the fake shoulder injury became a favorite in their household, the kind of story they imagined they'd tell their kids one day when they wanted to teach them about persistence, and maybe a little bit of creative problem-solving.

〜〜〜〜〜〜

The slam of the trunk brought Ricki back to the present. "Ready to go? I really don't want to hit traffic. I hate traffic," Anthony said, turning the key and slowly backing out of the driveway.

They hit the road. A few minutes into the drive, as he eased onto the expressway, Anthony asked, "What do you think this place will be like?"

"I don't know," Ricki said thoughtfully, tucking a strand of hair behind her ear. "The website makes it look beautiful, cozy, quiet, close to the water. And there's so much to do in the area: cute shops, restaurants to try, and great hiking trails I read about.

I think it's going to be a nice little vacation." She paused, her voice turning serious. "But I want to be really intentional about coming away from this experience with a new plan. I want to go back to the office in a few days and be excited again—like, *really* excited about what we're doing. I want to walk in there with a solid understanding of our 'why.' Does that make sense?"

Anthony nodded, gripping the steering wheel a little tighter. "It does. I've been thinking about that a lot too. You know, the other day I was remembering how excited and meticulous we were when we first thought about this business. We had notebooks and spreadsheets everywhere, trying to keep everything organized. I still remember waking up in the middle of the night and finding you hovered over your laptop, crunching numbers."

Ricki laughed. "I wasn't hovering. I was . . . diligently planning."

"You were obsessing like always," Anthony corrected with a grin. "But in the best way. And I think that's what made us such a good team back then. We had a plan, and we actually wrote down our goals. We were so determined to make it work. I miss that energy, you know? I feel like somewhere along the way, we got caught up in just *maintaining* instead of building. Like we were running the business, but now the business is running *us*."

Ricki nodded slowly, her expression softening. "You're right. When we started, we had so much drive. We'd talk for hours about how we wanted to grow and the kinds of lives we wanted to build, not just for ourselves, but for the people we'd eventually hire, too. We were so clear on our goals and roles back then."

"And now?" Anthony prompted.

"Now . . ." She sighed. "I feel like we've let the day-to-day grind take over. There are so many little fires to put out, so many decisions to make, that we've stopped dreaming. Or at least I have."

Anthony glanced at her, his jaw tightening with resolve. "That's what this trip is for. We'll get back to dreaming. We'll figure out how to make this business exciting again, not just something we do to pay the bills. And we'll make a plan for whatever's next."

Ricki smiled, the determination in his voice reigniting a spark in her. "Okay. Let's do it."

"First step," Anthony said, a teasing edge in his tone. "Finding that little coffee shop you bookmarked. I could use some caffeine before we start dreaming up a multimillion-dollar expansion plan."

Ricki laughed again, lighter this time. "Deal. But only if they have cinnamon rolls."

|||||||||||

After cinnamon rolls and coffee, Anthony sped down the highway and started to settle into a driving zone like it was Formula 1. Anthony loved to accelerate and drive fast even though Ricki hated it, but she was content to let him be a speed racer if it would make him happy. She needed Anthony to keep her balanced, and Anthony needed her to stay focused. This wasn't just going to be a getaway—it was going to be a turning point. She could feel it.

Anthony accelerated fast on the road for about an hour, and all was good. Until it wasn't. The flow slowed on the highway and turned into a slow-moving parking lot. He didn't have to say a thing; Ricki could see the disappointment written all over his face. He was hoping it was just an accident that would clear up soon, but the GPS was clear: It would be white-knuckle all the way to the Vineyard. As they sat in bumper-to-bumper traffic, tension began to creep back into the car. A ding of a text message interrupted their road trip playlist. Ricki picked up her phone, glanced at the screen, and let out a frustrated sigh.

"What is it?" Anthony asked, glancing her way briefly before turning his eyes back to the slowly creeping road.

"It's from Crystal at the shop," Ricki said, her tone sharp, paraphrasing it for Anthony. "Molly Stormsen is really mad. Said we told her that the brake replacement in her SUV would be done two days ago, and it's not. She's there and threatening to leave a bad review unless we can find a solution immediately."

Anthony frowned. "That doesn't sound right. I saw it on Hector's sheet earlier this week. I told him to prioritize that because she brought her other car in a few months ago and we dropped the ball on a repair, so I wanted to make sure we didn't mess this one up too. How *did* we mess this one up?"

"Great question," Ricki said, her voice rising. "Because when I checked earlier this week *and* yesterday, you said we were on track to have everybody serviced and out of there. Guess not."

Anthony sighed. "Maybe Crystal gave Molly the wrong date that it was going to be complete?" Anthony suggested.

Ricki turned in her seat so she was facing him, her frustration evident. "Anthony. Crystal is good at her job. If Hector told her when the job would be done, she would have communicated that clearly to Molly. The problem is not with her—it's with your insistence on always checking in with people instead of actually making sure the work gets done. And then I have to come in and deal with mad Molly and smooth it all over."

"Well, maybe if you weren't so worried about micromanaging everybody and doing everybody's job for them, there wouldn't be so much chaos or confusion," he replied flatly.

Ricki laughed. "Micromanaging? Is that what you call it when I go around and clean up everybody's mess? Is it micromanaging when I pick up the slack for people who can't seem to do their job? Is it micromanaging when I have to explain to a client that the reason that their car wasn't repaired on time was because you moved everything around in the shop without telling anyone and nobody knew where anything was? Is that what you mean by micromanaging?"

"All right. That's how we do this. We run into an issue, and you immediately find a way to blame me. You're the only one that knows what they're doing and all of us minions are just messing it all up, right? But let's not forget that you've made some pretty big mistakes too, Ricki."

Out of the corner of his eye, Anthony could see the rage bubbling up in her eyes. "Are you serious right now? I spend all day, every day, going behind you and a lot of the people at the store, fighting fires and fixing problems and making sure that you actually *do* what you say you're going to do. And you want to point your finger at *me* about my mistakes?" She laughed again, and Anthony knew that laugh very well. It meant this conversation was far from over, and that he would be hearing about it for a while.

The excitement that they had for this trip evaporated, the atmosphere in the car turned to frustration and resentment. Ricki could see Anthony clench and unclench his jaw as he crept forward in traffic, the tension between them palpable.

After a while of awkward silence, Ricki spoke up. This time she was quiet, but there was still a tone of seriousness in her voice "This isn't how I wanted our weekend to go. I was excited about getting away and figuring this out together. I didn't want to start it out yelling and blaming each other. I wanted to get back on the same page, but it doesn't even feel like we're in the same book." Anthony heard the sadness behind the anger.

He exhaled and thought carefully about what he wanted to say. He wasn't ready to smooth things over yet, but he also didn't want to add fuel to the fire. "Well, it's hard to be on the same page when all we do is look for each other's faults," he said quietly, and then, even though he knew it was a bad idea, added: "And if you didn't take so long checking and rechecking your work emails, we wouldn't be in this traffic."

Ricki, who had been trying to offer an olive branch, immediately crossed her arms and shifted her body toward the window, as if trying to get as far away from Anthony as she could.

"Excuse me for trying to make sure we didn't leave our practically failing business worse off than it already is," she said, tone ice cold. "I apologize for being the only one who seems to take the time to make sure things are done right," she added sarcastically.

"I'm not saying it's a bad thing that you care about the state of our business. But you act like perfection is the only option.

Sometimes good enough has to be good enough. And if you trusted me and the team to do what we are there to do, I bet more would get done. And we'd have less conversations like this." He gestured between the two of them.

"Trust you? Like how I trusted you to do the payroll on time and everybody's checks were late? Trust you like that?"

Anthony exhaled again. "We're not getting anywhere. Let's just stop."

"Yeah. Let's," she huffed.

||||||||||||

As traffic crept along, Ricki noticed that Anthony kept glancing at the time. She knew he was mentally calculating how long it would take them to get to Woods Hole Terminal, and debating whether or not they were going to miss the ferry. Ricki pulled up the ferry schedule on her phone and said calmly, "If we miss the noon ferry, the next one leaves at one forty-five. It'll be fine." He smiled, but she could tell it was an irritated smile. Not only was he annoyed that they were probably going to miss the ferry, but he was irritated that she knew him so well and could see that he was mentally spiraling.

As 11:00 turned to 11:30 and they still weren't at the terminal, they both silently resigned themselves to the fact that they were going to miss the ferry. "I'm sorry I took so long getting ready. I really tried to get out of there quickly," Ricki said quietly. Anthony huffed and shook his head slightly.

"We didn't *need* to go back to see Yolanda. We were there *yesterday*. Nothing has changed. And you know how she likes to chat."

"I couldn't stomach the idea of just leaving her like that. Especially when we know the drama and tension that she's dealing with. I wanted to let her know that we're on her side, and give her some tips on how to deal with the conflicting personalities of the managers. I just wanted to pop in and make sure she knew that we heard her."

Anthony nodded but stayed silent.

"I said I was sorry," Ricki continued. "I wanted to get out of there quickly too. I just felt like it was a loose end I needed to tie up before I could really relax for this trip. It's not like I wanted to miss the ferry."

They made small talk until it was their turn to drive onto the ferry. This part always made Ricki a little nervous, the idea of driving her car onto a boat, parking precariously close to other cars. But she took a deep breath and let her body relax. Even though they had argued about trust earlier, she realized that she always felt safe when Anthony was behind the wheel. He was a good driver, and she trusted him even at his high speeds. *I do trust him,* she thought. *So why do I have so much trouble letting go?*

By the time they arrived in Oak Bluffs and were back in their car, the tension had all but dissipated. They were holding hands again, laughing and talking about their vacation, and making observations about the gorgeous scenery all around them. Ricki had even opened up a little bit, trying to explain to Anthony why she felt such a pressure to have everything so perfect. She struggled to put it into words, but eventually was able to explain that her father had made owning and running a business look so effortless, and that she really wanted to live up to that. She explained that she didn't mean to drive him crazy with all of her micromanaging and attention to detail and perfectionism, but something about always working hard to be the best made her feel closer to her dad. This time, she could tell that Anthony was really listening to her. She plugged the address of the bed and breakfast into the GPS and decided that she was leaving all of the fights and arguments and issues back in Brooklyn and that this was the first step toward their new normal.

> *Take action! An inch of movement will bring you closer to your goals than a mile of intention.*
>
> —Steve Maraboli, *Unapologetically You*

ACTION STEP

Plan a getaway that allows you to disconnect from work and immerse yourself in a new environment. Whether it's a short retreat or an extended sabbatical, stepping away can rejuvenate your mind, boost creativity, and prepare you for the transformative steps ahead in your business journey.

CHAPTER 4

THE WELCOME RETREAT
Checking Inn for Clarity

Finally, after a long and tense day of travel, Anthony turned the car down a long gravel road lined with red maple trees. The car slowly crunched along the gravel until they rounded the corner and a gorgeous Victorian home came into view, standing proudly against the backdrop of the clear autumn sky.

The house stood three stories tall, with crisp white siding and accents of soft seafoam green on the shutters and intricate trim. A wraparound porch stretched across the front, adorned with wicker furniture, plump cushions, a porch swing, and hanging flower baskets that added pops of color. The peaked roof was topped with a charming weathervane, and bay windows on either side of the porch offered glimpses of cozy, inviting interiors.

In front of the house, a neatly manicured garden spilled over with dahlias, zinnias, and the occasional sunflower, their colors complementing the vibrant reds and golds of the surrounding trees. A stone pathway wound through the garden, leading to the front steps where two rocking chairs and a small table invited visitors to sit and take in the peaceful scenery.

"Wow," they said together as the car came to a stop. They both sat there for a minute, taking in the gorgeous architecture and stunning scenery that seemed to go on forever. Just then, a plump older lady with shoulder-length gray hair came bouncing through the screen door and started waving from the porch. Ricki could see that her apron had cats on it, and that she had a little bit of flour on her cheeks. Anthony gave Ricki a look, and they both instantly forgot about the painfully long and annoying ride. She knew that look well—it meant *Let's do this*. They both got out of the car and walked toward the front porch.

"You must be Anthony! Ricki! We're so glad you're here!" The woman greeted them enthusiastically. "Your sister Penny is such a doll, and we were thrilled to hear that you were coming to stay with us! Come in, come in. I'm Edna. We were expecting you hours ago. You guys must have run into traffic and missed the ferry?"

They glanced at each other, not wanting to spoil this moment with memories of the tense car ride. "Guess we didn't plan it very well," Ricki apologized. "We had a lot going on."

Edna thought about explaining that the website gave clear instructions for guests on best practices for a pleasant drive, how to avoid traffic, and how to make sure to catch the ferry up to the Vineyard, but the couple looked tense. She chose to leave it alone.

Anthony walked around to the trunk of the car to get the luggage, but Edna quickly waved him off. "No, no, come on in! You must be so tired and thirsty from your long drive. Trixie will bring your luggage up to the Tulip Room for you. I have sweet tea, lemonade, and if you drink beer there are a few cold ones in the cooler."

Before Anthony could respond, a surprisingly strong-looking brunette emerged from behind the house, walking with purpose toward the car. Without a word, she popped the trunk, grabbed both suitcases, and heaved them out as if they weighed nothing more than a couple of feather pillows.

Anthony frowned, taking a step toward her. "Oh no, no, I can take those," he said, reaching for the luggage.

Please don't make this a thing, Ricki thought, shooting him a subtle look. *Just let Trixie take the luggage. Don't make it weird.*

But Anthony's jaw was set, his discomfort plain to see. Ricki could practically hear the thoughts running through his head: The idea of someone else, especially a woman, carrying his bags for him made his shoulders stiffen. She'd seen this reaction before, a little flash of resistance in situations that challenged his sense of manhood.

He stood there awkwardly for a moment as Trixie, unfazed, hefted the bags up onto her shoulders with practiced ease. "Happy to help," she said with a cheeky grin. "I've got it." Then, with a wink, she turned and strode confidently toward the house, the suitcases bouncing lightly against her back.

Anthony looked at Ricki, a half-defensive, half-bewildered expression on his face.

"It's fine," Ricki said, patting his arm gently. "Let her do her thing."

He exhaled, still visibly uneasy, and followed her toward the house. As they climbed the porch steps, Ricki thought about the subtle ways Anthony's need to prove himself had woven itself into their lives over the years. She remembered how he always insisted on driving, even when he was exhausted, or how he would practically race to grab the check whenever they went out to eat.

Maybe it was his athlete's mindset, she mused, the identity he'd built around being strong, capable, and dependable. Masculinity had been such an integral part of who he was, especially during his football years. Even now, years later, that mindset lingered in moments like this. Ricki couldn't decide if it was endearing or exasperating. Maybe a little of both.

As they reached the front door, the woman beamed at them again, holding it open. "Come on in, and let's get you settled. Trixie will have your bags upstairs in no time."

Anthony hesitated, glancing back toward the car, but Ricki nudged him gently inside. "Just enjoy it," she said softly, her tone light but teasing. "It's not every day someone else carries your luggage."

He gave a small, sheepish chuckle, the tension easing slightly, and followed her into the charming foyer. But Ricki knew this moment would stick with him, an invisible tug-of-war between the man he was and the one he still felt he needed to be.

Ricki and Anthony followed Edna into the kitchen, a sunny yellow space with big windows overlooking the yard. A large rectangular table was the centerpiece, and locally inspired artwork hung in frames on the wall. One frame in particular caught Ricki's attention. It was a framed piece of cross-stitch, with flowers around the border and loopy script in the middle that read:

> *A dream written down with a date becomes a goal.*
>
> *A goal broken down into steps becomes a plan.*
>
> *A plan backed by action makes your dreams come true.*

Edna gestured for them to take a seat. "I'm not sure if your sister told you, but I'm Edna, and this," she said, gesturing around the meticulously clean kitchen, "is my playground. When I first had the idea of a bed and breakfast, the breakfast part of it was my main focus. I love to serve people and I love to cook, and I hope you will join us down here for breakfast each morning. Tomorrow I'll be making my famous blueberry pancakes, and every morning we will have a spread, and a variety of homemade muffins and biscuits to choose from. We'll have light snacks and appetizers available throughout the day, but breakfast is my specialty. It will be ready by seven-thirty sharp, so you can come down and we can eat and socialize for a little bit with our other guests and then you can be on your way to do whatever it is you came here to do." She moved seamlessly throughout the kitchen as she spoke, stirring pots, rinsing off dishes, and pouring them each a glass of ice water in a mason jar. "Don't miss breakfast and please don't be late. Our breakfast meetings are a treat and are very different."

"Thank you so much," Anthony said as he sipped his water. "We are so excited to be here. And blueberry pancakes sound great. You guys won't run out of pancakes, will you?"

"No, I don't believe in that. Trust me, you will have as many as you like. So, what brings you two lovebirds here? A little romantic getaway?" Edna asked as she put a plate of warm cookies on the table.

Anthony said, "I hope so," at the same time that Ricki said, "Kinda, but not exactly," and Edna looked back and forth between them in confusion.

"We actually own a business, and we came here to get away from it for a little while and do some thinking and planning," explained Ricki. "We haven't recalibrated our business in a long time, and we figured we could do it best in a new location. So that's our main focus, but we do plan to enjoy the sights around Martha's Vineyard while we're here."

"That's great," said Edna. "You're in the right place for that. I know firsthand the struggles and challenges that come with running a business with your partner. Coach should be here any second, and he can attest to that as well. We both loved our jobs, but when we hit retirement age we knew we wanted to do something completely different. He comes from a sports background and I come from a teaching background, and we really struggled to find a way to create something where both of us could shine."

"You found it in a bed and breakfast?" Anthony asked.

"We didn't find it. We created it. And it wasn't easy, I will be the first to tell you that. There's so many different dynamics going on when you're trying to run a business and still maintain a happy and loving marriage." Edna laughed. "And we're not perfect at it, but we've been at this for a long time and have learned a lot. Coach loves to share a lot of these insights with our guests, so along with blueberry pancakes tomorrow I'm assuming you'll get some wisdom about business and relationships from him, whether you want it or not!" Edna chuckled again, warmly.

"But he's a good listener, too," Edna continued. "So if you need advice or just a friendly ear, he's always around. He's a former high school football coach, and he can't help but coach. I tell him, 'Stanley, these guests are not your football team,' but poor guy—he can't help himself. Coaches coach, I guess. But the funny thing is, because of him, many of our guests who own a business come back annually not just for pancakes but to *talk* to Stanley. Penny comes a lot by herself."

Anthony smiled, clearly intrigued. "That sounds like it could be useful," he said, leaning forward slightly. "We're definitely at a point where we need to step back and figure out how to balance everything better. It's easy to get caught up in the grind, and sometimes it feels like we're losing sight of why we started in the first place."

Ricki nodded, glancing over at him with a knowing look. "Exactly. It's been hard to carve out time for ourselves, let alone focus on the big picture without the day-to-day chaos creeping in."

"Well, you're in good company," Edna said, voice warm and reassuring. "Coach and I faced those same challenges. Starting a new chapter later in life isn't without its bumps, but we've managed to make it work. We had to learn how to communicate differently, set boundaries, and trust that we both brought something important to the table. It's about finding balance—and a bit of humor along the way."

"I think we could use some of that humor," Anthony said with a smile, grateful for Edna's openness. "It's been a bit tense lately. But that's part of why we're here, right? To take a step back and get some perspective."

"You're doing the right thing," Edna said. "Sometimes you just need to hit pause and change the scenery. A fresh start, even if it's just for a few days, can make a world of difference. You never know what ideas will come to you when you allow yourself the space to breathe. Coach is always talking about fundamentals. He's a stickler for fundamentals and executing the playbook. He speaks in a sports language—some people get it right away, and others take a while."

"I like Coach already! And since we're both athletes," Anthony said, gesturing to himself and Ricki, "we're all about sports analogies!"

The room was quiet for a moment until the screech of the screen door caught their attention. Ricki turned toward the sound, hearing a few heavy footsteps before a mountain of a man filled the doorway. He exuded the kind of presence that came from years of commanding attention on a sideline. The first thing she noticed were his well-loved tennis shoes, permanently marked with grass stains and wear from countless summers. His khaki pants were complete with a skinny brown belt, just barely managing to support the slight beer gut that hung over it. A black polo shirt stretched comfortably across his broad shoulders, and his dark hair, still thick but streaked with silver, was combed neatly, giving him an air of casual authority. It was the same dorky but lovable style that many of her high school coaches had adopted. Coach looked like someone's kindly grandpa, yet there was something unmistakably familiar about his demeanor: the confidence, the charisma, and the subtle ease with which he surveyed the space. And he actually had a whistle around his neck. *Are you serious? This is weird. Why does this old man have a whistle around his neck? And does his wife call him Coach too? This is either going to be a great experience or the weirdest ever.* The thoughts ran through Ricki's head like a freight train.

"Why, hello there!" he boomed as he moved through the kitchen and came up behind Edna, who was busy washing dishes in the sink. He wrapped his arms around her, kissed her on the cheek, and then turned his attention back to the table.

"It's nice to meet you. I'm Stanley, but everyone calls me Coach," the big man said, holding out his hand to shake Anthony's. But he stopped mid-sentence, tilting his head slightly as if trying to place a familiar face. His brows furrowed, then lifted, the gears visibly turning in his mind.

"Wait a minute," Coach said, his eyes narrowing with recognition. "Are you Anthony Clark? From Liberty High School in Georgia?"

Anthony stood, a grin spreading across his face as he reached out to shake the coach's hand. Anthony poked out his chest, grinning from ear to ear.

"Yes, sir! Now, how do you know *me*?" Anthony said, still pumping the man's hand.

"Oh, I know all about Touchdown Tony," Coach said with a knowing grin. "I followed your career from high school, college, and, of course, the NFL. You were a hell of a running back. Fast and strong, with great vision. I was the coach at Century High School."

Anthony's face froze, the surprise evident in his expression as the realization hit.

Century High. The small-town underdogs who had pulled off the impossible. They'd beaten Liberty in the state championship, the only game Anthony's team lost that season. Ricki was slowly picking up on what was happening, and a lump instantly appeared in her throat. That loss still irked Anthony to this day. But Ricki had confidence they were at the right place, not only for themselves as business leaders, but also because she felt that Anthony may finally have found a person that could help him confront his demons.

Many still called it the biggest upset in Georgia high school football history. Touchdown Tony, the unstoppable force, had been completely shut down by a scrappy group of farm kids. He didn't score a single touchdown and the local media blamed him for the loss. Anthony had secretly carried that guilt until this day. Ricki was the only person on Earth that knew his dark secret.

"The one and only TDT . . . Touchdown Tony," Coach continued with a booming laugh, giving Anthony's hand a firm shake. "Quite the surprise. I heard your name more times than I can count back in my other life. You were a force to be reckoned with on that field! Son, you kept me up late at night trying to figure out how to not just stop you but how to contain you. But my guys got it done for me—we held Touchdown Tony scoreless!"

Ricki cleared her throat gently, pulling their attention back to her. Both men turned toward her, Anthony still looking a bit sheepish and stunned.

"Oh, I'm so sorry," Anthony said quickly, his tone slightly embarrassed. "This is my wife, Ricki."

Coach's demeanor softened instantly, his broad grin turning warm and welcoming as he extended his hand toward her. "Ricki, it's such a pleasure to meet you. I'm so glad you're here."

"Anthony talks about that game all the time. This is crazy. So you guys kind of knew each other?" Ricki asked, shaking his hand.

Coach chuckled. "Well, we didn't know each other directly, but I knew *of* him. Back when I was coaching high school football, Anthony's name was one you couldn't ignore. The kind of player who made you rethink your entire strategy. The best running back I have ever seen play high school football. Nobody thought we had a chance to win that game, but I knew we could. We created a game plan, and I knew if my farm kids executed that plan, we would win. We just had to stop your husband."

Anthony grinned from ear to ear at the compliment. "Coach here was a legend on the sidelines," he added. "He was one of the best high school football coaches, and his defense was one of the toughest we ever went up against. I think I still have bruises from that game. Your players were small, but man, did they tackle well and play great gap defense, and swarm to the ball, too."

Coach let out a hearty laugh, patting Anthony on the shoulder. "That was one hell of a game. We drilled fundamentals into those small farm kids, and they listened." Ricki noticed that a true bromance had been ignited. "But enough about football. What brings you two to my little corner of the world? And quite later than expected! You must have missed the ferry."

Edna looked at Ricki apologetically. Coach hated for his players to ever be late to anything, and he saw their guests as players on his mythical football team. It was his job to make them better. And he took his job seriously.

Anthony glanced at Ricki, their earlier tension easing slightly in Coach's presence. Anthony had renewed confidence in the vacation and saw Coach not just as someone who knew him but someone he could relate to.

"A little mix of work and relaxation," Ricki explained. "We run a business together and thought a change of scenery might do us good."

"Well, you've come to the right place," Coach said, his smile widening. "And who knows? Maybe we'll get a chance to swap a few more stories while you're here. I might even dig out some old game tapes if you're feeling nostalgic!"

"Coach has a copy of the famous upset and watches it once a year just for fun," Edna said, smiling at Ricki with a knowing glance. She, too, knew what it was like to be married to an athlete.

Ricki laughed. "Careful, Coach. He might take you up on that."

Coach winked. "You'd be surprised how many old athletes come through here looking for a trip down memory lane."

"These cookies are delicious, Ms. Edna—thank you," Ricki said, holding up the soft brown cookie.

"I'm glad you like them. When you're ready, you can head up to the room to settle in. It's just up those stairs—take a right, and it's the first door on your right. Take a little rest or get settled in if you want. That's a brand-new mattress up there in the Tulip Room. We'll be puttering around here the rest of the evening and can answer any questions you may have. Our friend Ronnie owns a cute little waterfront restaurant up the street—amazing clam chowder. I'd recommend that for dinner if you're hungry."

"Yes, please make yourselves at home," Coach added, reaching down to grab the last cookie off the plate.

"I think I will go upstairs and freshen up and rest a little bit. Long day," Ricki said, standing up from the table.

"I'll be up in a sec, babe—I'd like to chat with Coach for a bit," Anthony said, then looked over at Coach. "If that's okay with you, of course." Anthony had clearly found a new source of energy and intrigue in Coach.

Coach's face lit up. "Yes, I'd love that. Let's take a walk." Coach stepped out of the doorway and gestured for Anthony to lead the way.

As Anthony and Ricki stood to leave the kitchen, Ricki smiled and said, "Thank you again for the warm welcome. It's been such a pleasure meeting you, Stanley."

Coach grinned, his hands resting comfortably on his hips. "Stanley? No, no, please—call me Coach. Everyone calls me Coach."

Ricki raised an eyebrow. "Even here? At the bed and breakfast?"

"*Especially* here," Coach replied with a chuckle. "Doesn't matter if it's football players, guests, or my wife. 'Coach' just stuck. It's who I am."

"Well, thanks, Coach. We'll see you at breakfast tomorrow."

"Bright and early," Coach said, giving her a little salute. "It's served at seven-thirty sharp."

Ricki walked up the wooden staircase, the old boards creaking slightly under her feet, and made a right. The door to the Tulip Room stood out with its soft yellow paint and a beautifully hand-painted tulip in the center, a delicate reminder of the room's name. She turned the brass knob and stepped inside, immediately hit by a soft, inviting fragrance that smelled like a comforting mix of clean laundry and freshly picked flowers.

The king-size bed was the centerpiece of the room, positioned against the far wall beneath a framed painting of a blooming tulip field. The bed was covered in a crisp white duvet dotted with tiny yellow tulips, paired with fluffy pillows that practically begged her to sink into them. On either side of the bed stood small oak night-stands, each with a vintage brass lamp and a charming ceramic vase holding a single fresh tulip.

Near the window, an oak writing desk with a matching chair offered a cozy spot for journaling or planning. The desk had a few neatly arranged stationery items and a small, leather-bound guest book filled with handwritten notes from previous visitors.

The spacious closet featured sliding doors with full-length mirrors that reflected the natural light pouring in from the large window. Ricki approached the window and pulled back the pale yellow curtains, revealing a stunning garden view.

The Tulip Room felt like a perfect blend of charm, comfort, and a touch of romance, a space designed to make guests feel completely at home. Ricki took off her shoes and climbed into the large bed. She lay still for a while, looking up at the ceiling and listening to the sounds coming from downstairs, and quieted her mind just enough to relax into the handmade custom bed. It felt like she was being hugged by the warm blanket.

||||||||||||

Meanwhile, Anthony and Coach walked out to the front porch and sat down in the two rocking chairs. At first they made small talk about the drive from Brooklyn, the traffic, the ferry, and the weather, but their conversation quickly shifted to football.

"I always like to ask former athletes and coaches how they are adjusting to the real world after being so immersed in sports," Coach said, looking at Anthony. "I find that some guys transition easily while others find it hard to figure out who they are when they're in the real world. For me, it was a challenge, going from being a star player to being a coach. It's a whole different mentality. And then when coaching was over and we moved here to do this—" He gestured to the front porch. "I kind of had to reinvent myself. I had to relearn who I was and what I liked to do and figure out how to make that work so that Edna's dream could work. Our plan was for me to have career as a coach, and then we would retire to her bed and breakfast. That was our dream. Or, as I liked to call it, our audacious goal. And we did it."

"An audacious goal? I've never heard it worded like that before," said Anthony. "You know, I was curious about that. Coach, you didn't just have a career—it was legendary. How did a legendary coach like you end up running a bed and breakfast on Martha's Vineyard? Doesn't seem like the two—"

"Connect?" Coach asked.

"Yeah. Like, if your whole life has been dedicated to football, how do you just turn that off and decide that you want to explore the world of hospitality? Aren't you bored? How do you take your strengths and experiences from the field and find a way to apply them here?" Anthony asked.

Coach leaned back in his rocking chair, his eyes scanning the horizon as if searching for the right words. He rubbed his chin thoughtfully before turning back to Anthony.

"It's an important question because it's something every athlete, every coach, every person who's dedicated their life to a singular passion, will face eventually," he began. "For me, the answer wasn't immediate or easy. When I retired from coaching, I'll be honest: I floundered for a while. I'd spent decades watching games and diagramming plays, mentoring young men, strategizing for every possible scenario. And then, suddenly, there were no games to plan for. No team is relying on me. I didn't know what to do with myself."

Anthony nodded, his own experiences as a former athlete mirrored in Coach's words.

"What helped me," Coach continued, "was realizing that my skills as a coach weren't confined to the football field. Leadership, problem-solving, systems, and team building—those don't go away just because you leave sports. I realized that I am in the people business, and people need coaching regardless of the type of organization you are leading. Edna and I sat down, just like you and Ricki are doing now, and asked ourselves some tough questions. What do we want the next chapter of our lives to look like?

What are we passionate about? How can we support each other's dreams? What is our strategy? What are our core values and what type of team do we need to build around us to win?"

He gestured again toward the porch, the house, and the garden beyond. "This. This was Edna's dream. She's always been a people person, loves to create a welcoming space. I got a lot of credit for being a great coach, but the truth is, I didn't do it alone. I had a great staff, great assistant coaches, great parents, and Edna never got the credit, but she was right there with me the whole time helping me run my program. I'll admit, running a bed and breakfast was never on my radar, but I realized my role as a coach didn't have to end. A coach is a teacher, and Edna and I are both teachers at heart. Now, instead of coaching a team on the field, I'm coaching us, this business, this partnership. I bring the structure, the discipline, the ability to think on my feet. And you know what? It's been more rewarding than I ever imagined. Over the years, we began to engage the guests who were also business leaders, and we gave advice. And it's become a thing. We are helping business leaders win. People think they're coming for the pancakes, but they leave brand new. I realized by winning with some small farm kids that if you have a playbook and you execute it . . . you can win."

Anthony leaned forward, his elbows resting on his knees. "I have two questions for you, Coach. How did you adjust? I mean, going from a role where people look up to you, where you're calling the shots, to . . . making beds and serving coffee?"

Coach laughed deep and hearty. "You learn humility real quick when you're unclogging a guest's toilet at two in the morning." Both men laughed at that, and Coach continued, his tone softening, "But seriously, it's about shifting your perspective. In football, my goal was always to serve the team, to bring out the best in each player. Here, it's the same thing. I'm still serving our guests, Edna, and this vision we built together, and she's the lead on this one. And let me tell you, there's a quiet satisfaction in that kind of service. And the smile and joy I see on Edna's face is worth it. She believed in my vision, and now I am returning the favor by believing in hers. And I washed uniforms and painted the fields for years. A lot of serving goes into coaching. A coach's job is to build their people into the best version of themselves and get the team to work together."

Anthony sat back, letting Coach's words sink in. "I guess that's what I'm trying to figure out. Ricki and I are partners in our business, but sometimes it feels like we're speaking two different languages. I'm all about the big picture, the work and the future, and I'm just trying to keep up with the day-to-day details and managing all the people and relationships. And I believe it should be fun too. It's hard to find that balance—to be honest, I have struggled to understand and define my role. As a running back, my job was easy: Just grab the football and find the endzone. But now . . ."

Coach nodded but looked a little puzzled. "It's not easy. Marriage is a partnership, just like any good team. And running a business together is similar to running with the ball. The stakes are high, and the pressure's constant. But here's the thing—you and Ricki bring different strengths to the table, just like an offense. It's a total team effort. The key is learning to appreciate those differences and figuring out how to complement each other and being comfortable being codependent. That's when the magic happens."

Anthony let out a deep breath. "I never thought about it like that."

"And although you tried not to, did you ever fumble the ball?" Coach asked. Anthony nodded. "When my guys fumbled, I would give it right back to them the next play. The important thing is to have a short memory, pick the ball back up, and keep moving forward toward the end zone."

"Okay, Coach, here is my second question—it has been nagging me my whole life, and please don't take this the wrong way. How did you *do* it? How did you and your little farm kids beat us?"

Coach chuckled and then said, "Son, don't take *this* the wrong way, but we studied you for hours, and we noticed that you didn't follow your blocking. When you tried to run the ball into the endzone, it seemed like you were trying to do it all yourself. It seemed like you relied on you and your talent and not the play your coach called. So we told our guys that and made sure everyone stayed in their gap. If you would have followed your blocks, we would have been creamed. We saw your tendencies and showed the kids on film, and we practiced it. We had a game plan, and our audacious goal was not to let Touchdown Tony see the endzone—not one time."

He stopped to think, then continued. "Each player was responsible for their gap and to swarm to the ball. The kids listened and bought in. I'd always tell them, 'You are where your feet are.' I was a legendary coach, and I didn't get my hands on many players with your ability. But my kids bought in, were coachable, and followed the playbook and made me who I was. They were the true heroes because they would execute.

"Now, many of my high school players are leaders because we taught them the importance of the fundamentals of football and how important it is to follow the game plan. That is all we focused on: teaching fundamentals, and making sure each knew the playbook and everyone executed their roles. It was not about me, it was about *we*. We had that plastered all over the locker room." Coach stopped for a second, thinking. Then he added, "To win, you have to have a clearly defined strategy. Everyone must be accountable to their roles. We called that shared fate. Do your job because we all share in the responsibility of the outcome. Those farm kids taught me a lot too. In fact, give me some coachable players, and I think I could beat just about anyone with our system," Coach said with confidence. "In fact, we had a no-cut policy. Players who didn't buy in or execute would quit the team on their own. We focused on culture, and the right players bought in, and the wrong players quit."

They sat in silence for a while, and suddenly the exhaustion of the day came over Anthony like a flood. He thanked Coach again for the good advice, popped his head into the kitchen to say thank you to Edna again, and followed the stairs up to the Tulip Room. He kicked off his shoes, joined his sleeping wife in the plush king-size bed, and was asleep before his head hit the pillow for a much-needed nap.

When he woke up a few hours later, the warm glow of the setting sun was flooding into the room. He noticed that Ricki's side of the bed was empty and heard soft conversation coming from downstairs. He looked out the window and saw Edna and Ricki talking together near the garden. It looked like Edna was pointing out different vegetables that were growing and walking Ricki through her gardening process. Anthony made his way downstairs and into the yard to join them.

"There he is," Ricki said, snaking her arm around his waist for a side hug. "Edna and I were just chatting, but she highly recommended we go check out her friend Ronnie's place. Are you hungry?"

"Starving," Anthony said, putting his hand to his stomach. Edna gave them basic directions to the waterfront restaurant, and they were refreshed and on their way.

They shared one of Ronnie's famous sauteed lobster rolls and a bowl of lobster bisque, then strolled the waterfront hand in hand, people-watching and popping into sidewalk boutiques along the way. They found their way to a local pub to watch tourists sing bad karaoke and try flights of local beers.

At one point during a lull in conversation, Ricki pulled her phone out of her purse and, without even thinking about it, opened the apps to check the cameras at all the offices. Checking in on the office was such a habit, she almost didn't realize she was doing it— and on this much-needed date.

"Nobody's there, babe." Anthony said softly, putting his hand on her arm. "Nobody back home needs you right now. There's nothing that needs to be done. Just be here, with me." He looked into her eyes.

Ricki's finger hovered over her email app, but she resisted and dropped her phone back into her purse.

Vision without action is merely a dream. Action without vision just passes the tie. Vision with action can change the world.

—commonly attributed to Joel A. Barker

ACTION STEP

Download or print the Vision Statement worksheet by scanning the QR code below.

Set aside quiet time to prayerfully reflect and write out your business vision, inspired by Habakkuk 2:2. Make your vision specific, clear, and compelling—something that will inspire you and your team to action. Post your written vision somewhere visible and review it regularly, using it as your North Star for decisions and daily focus. A vision made plain doesn't just clarify your path—it invites God's provision, aligns your team, and puts true, lasting success into motion.

CHAPTER 5

FROM DRIFT TO DIRECTION
The Power of Alignment

The next morning, Ricki and Anthony joined Coach and Edna in the sunlit kitchen for breakfast. They recalled their adventures from the night before, and thanked Edna for recommending Ronnie's. As they ate and talked, the sound of a car coming up the driveway drew their attention outside. Coach and Edna stood up and went out to the porch, and Ricki and Anthony followed. A large green Volkswagen van came to a stop in front of the porch, and Ricki saw that it was a "patchwork of personality," as her late grandfather would say when he came across something equal parts charming and chaotic. The van's sides were painted with a cheerful, hand-done mural of sunflowers and mountains, and it had a single bumper sticker that read: "Life Happens, Coffee Helps."

The driver got out and rushed around the front of the van to open up the passenger side door. Both driver and passenger were clean-cut and fit, the man with a few tattoos peeping out from his short-sleeve shirt and the woman with lime green cat-eye glasses and a messy bun. Edna stepped off the porch to greet them.

"Everyone, meet Nate and Clara!" Edna announced warmly.

The newcomers, in their late thirties, were all smiles as they introduced themselves. "We're sort of . . . on a journey," Nate explained vaguely, waving his hand in the air like he was sketching a cloud. "We're looking for the perfect town to start our dream business!"

"Oh, what kind of business?" Ricki asked, intrigued.

"A mobile coffee truck!" Clara said enthusiastically. "We're going to park in scenic spots and serve artisanal coffee with locally sourced pastries. Picture it: morning sunshine, great views, happy customers. It's going to be amazing."

"It does sound amazing!" Ricki said. "How long have you been working on it?"

Clara hesitated, glancing at Nate. "Well . . . we came up with the idea about six months ago," she said.

"Actually, eight," Nate corrected, chuckling.

"Right, eight," Clara agreed. "But, you know, we didn't want to rush into anything, so we decided to hit the road first. Scope things out. Let inspiration guide us."

The more Ricki listened, the more it became clear that while their dream was big, their approach lacked structure and detail.

Nate and Clara seemed to be floating from town to town, waiting for the perfect moment to magically appear instead of taking concrete steps to make it happen.

As the morning went on, the cracks in their plan became more apparent. Nate mentioned how they hadn't actually bought the coffee truck yet because they couldn't decide on the right model. Clara also admitted they hadn't settled on a budget, and when Ricki asked about permits or suppliers, they both laughed nervously. "We'll figure it out as we go," Nate said.

Ricki couldn't help but admire their optimism but also felt a pang of concern. Their lack of accountability to themselves, or to each other, was evident. Every question about logistics or next steps was met with vague answers or deflections. It was clear they had a vision but no real strategy or plan to bring it to life.

"Sounds like a bold plan," Coach said. "What's your timeline for getting the truck and launching?"

Nate looked at Clara and then fiddled with his wedding ring nervously. "We need to find the right truck. There's just so many choices. But we will know it when we see it," he said, finally making eye contact with Coach.

"And the budget?" Coach asked.

Edna swooped in. "Okay, okay, let's not interrogate them the moment they get in, huh? Let's get you inside. Trixie will get your luggage. Come have some breakfast and get settled in. You'll be in the Marigold Room," Edna said, gently ushering the newcomers into the house and shooting Coach a glance over her shoulder.

Coach shrugged. "Was just asking," he said with a smile to Ricki and Anthony. As the conversation turned to football, Ricki found herself digging in her purse again for her phone. She noticed she had one missed text message, from Yolanda.

Things got heated between the managers last night. Customers were around. Not good. Told them both not to come in today, so we're going to be short-staffed. Just wanted you to know.

Ricki sighed and Anthony and Coach turned their attention to her.

"Everything okay?" Anthony asked

"Not really. Turns out the managers at Yolanda's store got into it last night. Sounds like customers witnessed it. She told them not to come in today, so they're short-staffed." Ricki ran her hand through her hair. She and Anthony discussed what to do next for a while, and then Coach piped in.

"Sounds like you've got some big decisions to make. What's your plan?"

"Well, we have to fix the most important things first. This is going to turn into a reputation problem. Customers witnessed this, and that's going to get around fast. The last thing that Yolanda needs is more drama at that store. We need to take care of the short-staffing issue, maybe see if someone from the other store can cover a manager position today," Ricki suggested, looking at Anthony. He nodded.

"That sounds like a good way to fix the immediate problem, but this is a great opportunity to build a foundation for how you're going to solve problems like this in the future," said Coach. "How can you use this situation to put systems in place so that you don't have to put out this particular fire again?"

Ricki and Anthony looked at Coach blankly. "Before you even think about managing conflict out there, you've got to get aligned in here," he said, tapping the table between them.

"When the two of you aren't in agreement, no one else can be. Conflict at the top always trickles down. That's why, as leaders, you *must* get on the same page no matter how long it takes. You have to walk in agreement, or everything beneath you will keep falling apart. Coach softened his tone and continued, "You two aren't just running a business; you're shaping a shared legacy. When your minds align, you create momentum no challenge can stop."

He paused, then added, "The confusion and chaos in your company? It's just a reflection of the tension between you two."

Then, softly but firmly, he said, "Amos 3:3—*Can two walk together unless they are agreed?* If you two can align, everything else can follow."

"Let me call Yolanda and see how we can fix the short-staffing issue, and then maybe you and I can start brainstorming a plan so this doesn't happen again?" Anthony asked, standing up and taking his phone out of his pocket. "We need to find a way for us to get aligned before we can expect *them* to be aligned." He walked out of sight, leaving Ricki and Coach sitting in silence.

When he returned, Ricki was already tapping away on her laptop.

"So I started drafting a conflict management plan that we can use moving forward so things like this don't happen as often," Ricki said quickly. Anthony could tell by the way she was talking a mile a minute that she was excited. "So it starts with clearly defining roles—like actually writing them down, not just assuming everyone knows—and then I added a section about communication flow, like who talks to who and when, and a step-by-step system for addressing issues in real time . . . oh, and I should color code the priority levels—"

She stopped, and her fingers flew across the keyboard. "Green for low, red for urgent—and there's a section on follow-ups, like how we document outcomes, and—"

"Hold on." Coach's deep voice stopped her in her tracks. Ricki looked up, confused.

"A conflict management plan is a good idea. And definitely something you could work on later. But first, *you two* have to come to an agreement that you're going to be working this business in alignment. You have to be on the same page when it comes to how you're going to handle things between the two of you before you can even start to think about how you're going to handle things between everyone else."

Ricki's shoulders relaxed, and Anthony could tell she was a little disappointed that her idea for a conflict management plan had been met with some resistance.

"Wait right here," Coach said, heading inside. When he returned, he was holding a white piece of paper that had been folded and refolded many times. He handed it to Ricki, and she looked at him curiously as she unfolded it. Anthony moved behind her to read it.

"What is this?" Ricki asked.

"A few years ago," Coach explained, "I had a couple here that ran a home cleaning business. They had fancy vans with their logo on the sides, and a team of ten or so cleaners that worked for them all over the city. But they came here worried that their business wouldn't make it another year. There was a lot of confusion and miscommunication when it came to how things were done. They were getting more and more subpar reviews, they were losing customers, and it caused a lot of stress in their marriage. When they were here, Edna came up with this.

"It's a Partnership Agreement," Coach continued. "It's a way to get crystal clear about what you two can expect from each other and what you are promising to do moving forward. It's not about Yolanda or the other managers—it's about the two of you. When two people agree, anything can be done. You two have to get clarity in your purpose before anything else can happen."

Coach dug a pen out of his deep khaki pockets and put it on the table in front of them.

"You two take a minute to fill this out. Take your time and really think each question through. It covers your roles and responsibilities, how you'll make decisions, and it'll make it easier to be accountable to each other. I'll be over there if you need me." He winked at them and pointed to the garden.

Ricki and Anthony positioned themselves around the small bistro table and looked down at the document:

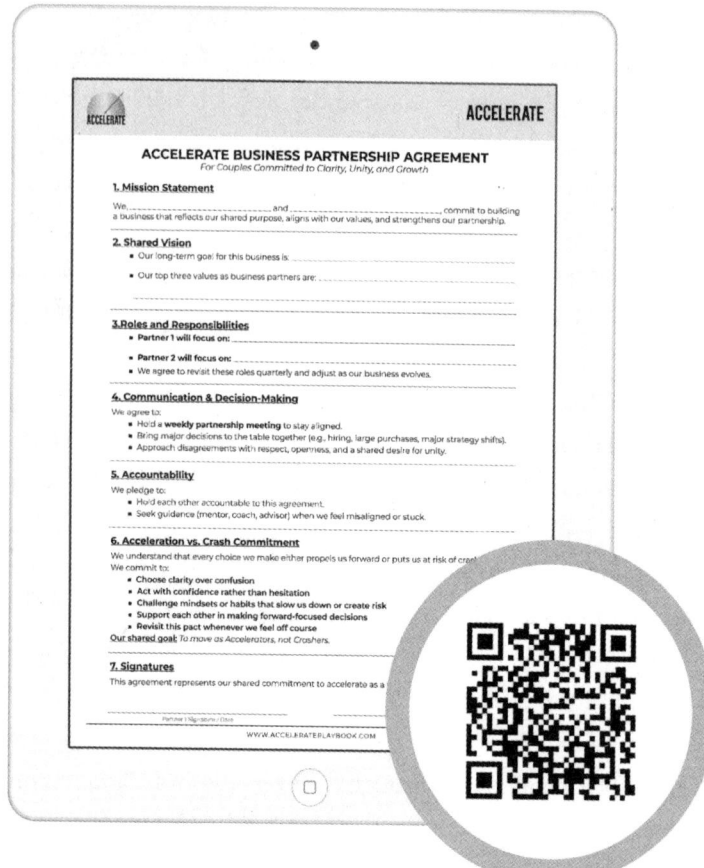

Over the next hour, they pored over the document, having deep and overdue conversations about purpose, time, habits, accountability, and running their business in faith instead of fear.

When Coach reappeared from the garden, sweaty and with dirt-covered hands, he looked over their shoulders to read what they had written. Ricki sat very still, waiting for Coach's response.

"This is great, guys. I love the weekly check-in questions, how you listed your top three values, and how you made it very clear who is responsible for what. I see this kind of like wedding vows. Promises you make to each other that you can refer back to when things are hard. This—" Coach pointed one dirty finger onto the paper. "This is what is going to keep you aligned. And when the two of you are aligned, you'll be unstoppable."

Coach went inside, and Ricki took a deep breath and smiled. With this clarity in front of her, she felt equipped to handle whatever came next. The rest of the evening was spent lazily relaxing on the porch, snacking on chips and homemade salsa made from the veggies in the garden.

Later that evening, Coach invited the two couples into the spacious backyard, where he had a glowing fire going in the firepit. Everyone found a seat around the fire, and speakers from the front porch sent smooth coffeehouse acoustic music through the air.

The sound of a car on gravel pulled their attention from the fire to the driveway as a sleek Mercedes-Benz came creeping into sight. "That must be David and Darla," Edna said, standing up from her chair and walking over to meet them. Ricki couldn't see or hear them very well, and was surprised that instead of coming over to join them, the couple simply grabbed their designer suitcases and made a beeline for the house.

Edna came back to the fire, looking confused. "They're tired. We'll introduce you to them later." It seemed a little odd, the way they arrived and quickly retreated, but Ricki knew what it was like at the end of a long travel day, just wanting to shower and get into bed.

Later that night in the Tulip Room, Ricki reflected on their conversation with Nate and Clara from earlier in the day. She realized that while spontaneity and dreaming big had their place, real progress required more than just hope. It required a solid plan, consistent action, accountability, and a willingness to make hard decisions.

When Anthony joined her in the bed, she shared her thoughts. "I admire their courage," Ricki said, "but it's like they're waiting for the universe to hand them their dream instead of going after it."

Anthony nodded. "It's a good reminder for us, too," he said thoughtfully. "Big ideas are great, but they don't mean much if there's no follow-through. We've got to hold ourselves accountable, for this trip and everything that comes after it. Coach was right— we are reactive and rarely proactive. I'll never forget this lesson. We should have taught our people how to communicate first. It would've reduced our conflicts."

Ricki started to add something else, but the sound of her husband's snoring let her know it was better to wait until the morning.

Don't cling to a mistake just because you spent a lot of time making it.

—commonly attributed to Aubrey de Grey

ACTION STEP

Review your current team and ask yourself:

Are your people in roles that match their natural strengths and interests?
Is anyone underutilized or overwhelmed?
What key responsibility are you holding on to that someone else could do better?

This week, choose one critical task or area to delegate to a team member whose strengths align with that responsibility. Clearly communicate your expectations, give them the authority to make decisions, and set a follow-up meeting to review progress. By recalibrating your team and empowering the right people, you'll free yourself to focus on growth and create a stronger foundation for your business.

CHAPTER 6

THE PLAYBOOK IMPERATIVE
Why Strategy Wins

The next morning, the inviting aroma of blueberry pancakes and freshly brewed coffee lured Ricki and Anthony downstairs.

"Good morning!" Edna greeted as she set a plate of steaming pancakes in the center of the table. "Sit, sit! We've got plenty of food and plenty to talk about. If we run out, I can make more."

Coach was seated at the head of the table, in the middle of an enthusiastic conversation, and his body language immediately reminded Ricki of her dad, the way he had his chair tilted back at an angle that seemed both relaxed and commanding. Across from him sat Nate and Clara, leaning forward as if trying to absorb every word. Coach had that tone, the one Ricki had heard before, firm but full of encouragement.

"—Because having a dream is great, but without a strategy, it's just a wish," he said, tapping the table lightly for emphasis. "You've got to ask yourself, what's the first step? The second? What happens if the wheels fall off the bus? Literally or figuratively."

Nate chuckled nervously. "We've been meaning to map things out a bit more."

Coach raised an eyebrow but softened it with a knowing grin. "*Meaning to* doesn't pay the bills, son. Start small. Write down three steps tonight. Doesn't matter if they're perfect, just get moving."

Clara nodded earnestly. "That makes sense. We've been so focused on the big picture that we kind of forgot the little stuff."

"That's the trick," Coach replied. "A good plan keeps you grounded, but it must be flexible. You don't have to figure it all out, but you've got to give yourself a road map. Otherwise, you're just hoping for the best and wandering wherever the wind blows. And life's wind? It's not always kind."

Ricki and Anthony lingered in the doorway, watching the interaction unfold. There was something mesmerizing about the way Coach could distill wisdom into simple truths, handing it out like candy while still making it hit like a brick. Nate and Clara soaked it up, their heads bobbing in agreement as if they were hearing these concepts for the first time.

That was when Coach noticed them lingering and waved them in. "There they are!" he said with a smile. "Come sit, coffee's hot. How'd you sleep?"

"Great!" they both said at the same time, finding their seats. Once they had big plates of blueberry pancakes in front of them, Coach cleared his throat.

"So, you two are here to strategize, huh? I love it. Nothing gets me going like a good game plan." He set his mug down and clapped his hands together. "Let's see what you've got."

Ricki blinked. "See what we've got?"

"Yeah, your plans, your playbook," Coach said, leaning forward. "You have a playbook, right? Or maybe you call it something else. Whatever documents you've been using to strategize, your goals, your analysis, your step-by-step for how to move forward. Show me the blueprint of how you roll as an organization. The first day of football practice, I always gave my players my playbook. Anthony, didn't you get a playbook on your football teams in high school and college?"

Anthony nodded, but then exchanged an uneasy glance with Ricki before clearing his throat. "Uh . . . we don't really have that."

Coach raised an eyebrow. "No playbook? Can I see your core values? Can I see your mission statement?"

Ricki shook her head, feeling a little embarrassed. "We've talked about things. Ideas, goals, but we've never written anything down formally. I mean, we used to—that was my jam back in the day. I was the queen of spreadsheets and planners and calendars and notebooks. But now, it feels like we've just been . . . winging it," she admitted.

"Planning can be exciting in the beginning," Coach agreed. "You're still pumped up and excited about this new adventure, and it makes you want to spend all of your time thinking and planning and dreaming. But then, when the newness wears off and you're up all night crunching numbers and learning how to run a business, the intentional planning and strategizing takes a back seat. Which leads to you just—"

"Winging it," Edna finished for him with a knowing smile.

Coach leaned back, his expression thoughtful. "Winging it. So dangerous," he repeated slowly. "Let me ask you something. Do you work hard?

"Yes, we do, so hard," Anthony said.

"So hard work is not your issue. Everyone works hard. Champions work with a purpose. Would you ever go into a game without a playbook, Anthony? No strategy? No well-executed plays to guide your team?"

Anthony immediately shook his head. "Of course not. That'd be crazy, chaotic."

"Exactly," Coach said, pointing at him. "Running a business isn't any different. If you don't have a plan, a playbook you follow, you're just hoping for the best. And hope—well, hope's not a strategy, is it?"

Ricki sighed. "You're right. We've been so caught up in the day-to-day that we haven't taken the time to actually put a plan together. My college soccer team, we ran plays, too." She set her coffee cup down slowly. "Coach," she said, "this might sound silly, but I told Anthony the other night—I think we've become Crashers."

Coach raised an eyebrow. "Crashers?"

"It's what we used to call people in the business world who didn't have a plan. They weren't steering—just reacting, running into the same walls over and over. We used to laugh about it when we saw it in others. But lately?" She glanced at Anthony. "We've been winging it, hoping effort alone will get us through."

Anthony nodded. "No GPS, no alignment—just pedal to the floor and hope we don't hit anything. That's how it's felt."

Coach didn't laugh. He nodded. "Sounds like you've already started doing the work. That's what naming it is. Once you recognize you're crashing, you can stop the car. Recalibrate. And drive with intention again."

Coach smiled warmly, his tone softening. He knew these former athletes would catch on quickly. "Don't beat yourselves up. You're not alone. A lot of people get so busy running the race, they forget to check the map. In fact, if you had followed our recommendations, you would have been on time yesterday instead of fighting through traffic." At this, Anthony looked down and sighed. "But that's why you're here. To stop, reassess, and chart a course forward. So let's start fresh." The vibe was feeling less like a traditional bed and breakfast and more like a corporate retreat.

The conversation shifted as breakfast was served. Over steaming cups of coffee and pancakes, Coach and Edna began to share their wisdom. Edna had a lot to offer too, and Ricki thought she should be called Coach 2.0. Throughout their conversation, Ricki learned that although Edna was not into sports, she understood structure and order because she'd played in the marching band, which required precision and coordination, *and* she had spent years as a chemistry teacher commanding her classrooms.

"Running this bed and breakfast taught us a lot about business. Planning is everything," Edna began. "When we first started, we didn't think we needed to write everything down either. But we quickly learned after six tough months that having clear goals and strategies kept us focused and helped us avoid unnecessary stress, so we recalibrated quickly."

Coach nodded. "And it's not just about writing things down for the sake of it. A good plan forces you to analyze. What's working? What's not? What's next? Those are the three questions Edna and I ask ourselves all the time. And we are constantly recalibrating. It took Edna twenty years to perfect her blueberry pancakes. She started working on the perfect recipe by feeding our players before every big game. In fact, they were full of pancakes when we stuffed Anthony in the backfield a few times." Coach laughed. Anthony was caught off guard by Coach's quick wit and subtle digs.

"What's working, what's not, and what's next. Got it," Ricki said, locking it into her memory. Anthony chimed in: "Recalibrate."

"Let me give you an example," Coach said. "When we started, our check-in process was a mess. Guests were waiting too long, and it was hurting their experience. Once we sat down, analyzed what was going wrong, and wrote out a new process, everything improved. Now, check-ins are smooth as butter and our survey reviews have improved drastically."

Edna chimed in, "And we do the same with guest feedback. I read every review, good, bad, and ugly. Those reviews are like a mirror, showing us where we shine and where we stumble. And once we see those patterns, we adjust. That's the power of a written plan. It helps you take what you learn and turn it into action. We noticed several of our guests would arrive late because of traffic, so we gave travel instructions through our website. For people who are planners, it's very helpful. Do you guys have customer reviews? And do you read them?"

Their blank stares were all Edna needed to understand the answer. *No benefit to hearing people complain,* Anthony had always thought.

Ricki and Anthony were quiet for a while, thinking about what Coach had said and enjoying the perfectly constructed pancakes, maybe the best they'd ever eaten. After a moment of quiet contemplation, Coach steered the conversation back to the purpose of the couple's visit.

"Here's the thing about making plans," he began, pouring syrup onto his plate. "You can't move forward until you've taken a good, hard look at where you've been. Every great journey begins by understanding what you're carrying with you. Sometimes, success is about knowing when to lighten your load or strengthen your resolve."

Ricki tilted her head, intrigued. "What do you mean by 'understanding what you're carrying with you'?"

Coach pointed his fork at her, his eyes twinkling. "Your past. The lessons you've learned, the mistakes you've made, the patterns you fall into without even realizing it. Your blind spots. All that stuff? That's your baggage. Some of it's helpful: skills, strengths, wisdom you've picked up along the way. But some of it? Deadweight. Fear, bad habits, insecurities, misplaced priorities. The key is figuring out which is which."

Edna chimed in, slicing into her pancake. "That's why reflecting on your past is so important. It's not about beating yourself up for what went wrong. It's about learning from it. For example, when we first started this place, we didn't listen to our guests as much as we should have. We were so focused on what *we* thought they wanted, we completely missed what they were actually telling us."

"What happened?" Anthony asked, genuinely curious.

Edna shrugged with a wry smile. "Guests started leaving reviews saying breakfast was great, but they wished we had more dietary options. Gluten-free, dairy-free, that sort of thing. At first, I was annoyed. Didn't they see how much effort we were putting in? But then I realized their feedback was a gift. We adjusted the menu, and guess what? Not only did the reviews improve, but so did our bookings. Reflecting on those early mistakes taught me to seek feedback, even the tough kind, as an opportunity instead of a criticism."

"Okay, reflecting on past experiences. We can do that. What's next?" Anthony asked.

But before Coach could answer, the sound of high heels coming down the stairs drew everyone's attention to the kitchen doorway. A second later, a tall, stunning woman with a short blonde bob and a commanding presence appeared. Her beige dress hugged her in all the right places, and her designer clutch fit snugly under her arm. She glanced around the room, her face expressionless. Just then, an equally handsome man appeared behind her, dressed in freshly pressed khakis, a polo shirt, and boat shoes. He, however, looked happy to be there. *They can't be over twenty-five*, Ricki thought to herself, and whispered discreetly to Anthony, "Daddy's money."

"Morning, everyone! I'm David. This is my fiancée, Darla," the young man said, walking around the table and pulling out a seat for his lovely bride-to-be. She sat, glancing at everyone with a tight smile.

"Well, hi there! Nice to meet you! Shame we didn't get to say hello last night," Coach said. Ricki wasn't sure if that was meant to be a dig or not. "What's your story?"

David looked a little uncomfortable before he answered. "Oh, us? No story. Just passing through," he said as he accepted a cup of coffee from Edna.

"Everyone's got a story!" Coach pressed.

"We're, uh, figuring some stuff out. We're from New Jersey, but . . ." He hesitated. "We're not sure if that's where we are supposed to be. So we're . . . figuring some stuff out," he said again.

Coach shot a glance at Edna, who shrugged. The vibe in the room was awkward, as people tried to start up conversations that seemed to go nowhere. Ricki noticed the woman, who still hadn't said anything, had only had a few pieces of fruit and a few sips of coffee. Ricki could feel the woman's knee bouncing under the table.

"Well," said Coach, "we were just talking a little bit about business, and I was just telling these folks about how important it is to assess your strengths and weaknesses. This is where a lot of people get stuck. They're either too hard on themselves, focusing only on their weaknesses, or they think they've got it all figured out and ignore their blind spots. Neither approach works. You've got to be honest and balanced."

"How do you figure out your blind spots if, well, they're blind spots?" Nate asked.

Coach grinned, clearly pleased with the question. "That's where feedback comes in. You ask people you trust: family, friends, mentors, people who see you from angles you can't see yourself. And you listen to them, even when it stings."

David's hands froze. Ricki could see the tension coming over his body, and his fiancée looked just as uncomfortable. David slowly put his coffee mug down, took his napkin off his lap, put it on the table, and stood.

"Hate to eat and leave, but we've got a meeting," David said, standing. Darla did the same. "Thanks for the breakfast," he added before taking Darla's hand. They quickly disappeared out of the kitchen and out the front door.

The kitchen was silent for a moment, everyone trying to process what had just happened. Coach shook his head and redirected his attention back to Nate, while Edna took off her apron and left the kitchen.

"Getting feedback from people you trust," Coach said, refocusing. "It shows growth. Feedback's no good if you don't act on it."

Coach's expression softened. "That's where self-awareness comes in. You've got to know your core values, what's most important to you. Advice is great, but it's your life. Use feedback to sharpen your own instincts, not to let others steer the ship."

Anthony, who had been quietly taking it all in, finally spoke. "So, it's kind of like football, right? You study the tape, figure out where you messed up, and listen to the coach. But at the end of the day, it's you on the field, making the plays."

"Exactly," Coach said with a nod. "And that's why reflecting on your strengths and weaknesses is so crucial. It's your game. Own it."

Anthony nodded. "So, how do we do that?"

"Start by asking yourselves some questions," Coach said. "What are you naturally good at? What comes easy for you? Those are your strengths. Then ask: What feels like a constant struggle? What do you avoid because it's hard or uncomfortable? Those are your weaknesses. And don't stop there. Think about your partnership, too. Are you both leaning into your strengths, or are you stepping on each other's toes? When we first started, we didn't divide responsibilities based on what we were good at. Edna was handling guest logistics, which is not necessarily her strong suit, and I was fumbling through social media marketing. Once we switched roles, everything clicked."

Anthony chuckled. "Yeah, Ricki and I definitely need to work on that."

Ricki shot him a playful look. "You mean you need to stop trying to do everything yourself?"

Movement from outside the kitchen window caught Ricki's attention. Edna was leaning into the driver's side window of the Mercedes, talking to the driver. After a few words, the car reversed, leaving Edna standing in the driveway. Ricki saw her take a deep breath and come back into the house.

Coach grinned. "Now you're getting it. Recognizing patterns and triggers is the next step. Take a look at where things tend to go wrong. Do you notice the same mistakes happening over and over? Are there certain situations or tasks that always seem to cause tension?"

Ricki paused, then asked, "You mean like how we always fight about logistics because I think he's too disorganized and he thinks I micromanage?"

"Bingo," Coach said, tapping the table for emphasis. "That's a pattern. And patterns don't break themselves. You've got to address the root cause and work together to change it."

Edna was leaning into the driver's side window of the Mercedes, talking to the driver. After a few words, the car reversed, leaving Edna standing in the driveway. Ricki saw her take a deep breath and come back into the house and walk quietly back into the kitchen.

Edna leaned in a little and turned gently toward Ricki. "You know, I wonder if your 'micromanaging,'" she said, using air quotes, "isn't really about control. I wonder if maybe it's about fear."

Ricki looked surprised, but Edna's tone stayed soft. "When we lead from fear—fear of failure, fear of things falling apart—we start thinking we have to hold everything together ourselves. That kind of pressure tricks us into thinking we're being responsible, when really, we're carrying more than we were ever meant to."

Coach leaned in, locking eyes with Ricki. "Ricki, I see it. That tight grip? That need to control everything? It's fear disguised as leadership. And that fear will choke your business. You have to let go of fear to let growth in."

Edna nodded and gave a kind smile. "But faith doesn't micromanage. Faith knows when to act and when to release. It trusts that when you build the right systems and surround yourself with the right people, you don't have to hover over everything to make sure it stays upright."

"Sometimes it's not even about the task; it's about how you communicate," Coach added. "If you can recognize your triggers and approach them with empathy instead of frustration, you'll make progress faster than you think."

The table fell silent for a moment as Ricki and Anthony absorbed the advice, the smells of syrup and coffee filling the air.

"So, what now?" Ricki finally asked.

Coach spread his hands with a grin. "Now, you take this knowledge and use it. Reflect on the past. Assess your strengths and weaknesses. Recognize those patterns. And then, you make a plan. Not a perfect plan, but one that's clear and actionable."

Edna leaned in, her voice warm. "And remember, don't forget to celebrate what's working. Even the small wins matter. They'll remind you why you're doing this in the first place."

Ricki and Anthony exchanged a look, both feeling a sense of clarity and determination they hadn't felt in months.

"Thanks," Anthony said, his voice sincere. "This was . . . exactly what we needed."

"Good," Coach said, finishing the last bite of his breakfast. "Because the game's just beginning. And trust me, you're going to crush it once you've got your playbook in order. And one last thing. There's a Bible up there in your room in one of the nightstands. If you want to know what another wise guy had to say about this, check out Habakkuk 2:2." He winked, stood up from the table, and brought his dishes to the sink.

"I'm headed out to the garden if you need me, sweetpea," he said to Edna, kissing her on the cheek. Anthony and Ricki stood up, too, bringing their dishes to the sink as well.

"We've got some bikes out there in the garage if you two want to enjoy the sunshine and ride along the water," suggested Edna, wiping her hands on her apron. "You could swoop into the cute little downtown area too, do some shopping or people watching. If you follow the path from the garage down around that way, it takes you right to one of the bike trails around here."

"Oh man, I haven't been on a bike in forever!" Ricki said, smiling like a schoolgirl.

"Let's do it!" Anthony said. "Thank you again for breakfast this morning, Ms. Edna. Pancakes were delicious."

"I'm glad you thought so! We'll be around all day if you need anything. Just go around the house this way," she pointed, "and you'll see them leaning up against the garage. Have fun!" she said as she turned back to the sink of dirty dishes.

Ricki turned toward the front porch, and Anthony touched her elbow. "I'm just going to run upstairs for something real quick. I'll meet you out there."

Ricki headed to the garage, and Anthony bounded up the stairs. Once he was back in the Tulip Room, he went straight for the nightstand on his side of the bed. He pulled out the Bible, and it immediately brought back memories of hard wooden church pews with his grandma, the little red candies she'd sneak to him so he'd stay quiet, and the unique smell of perfumes, sweat, and leather Bibles. He flipped through the pages until he found what he was looking for:

> **Habakkuk 2:2:** Write the vision; make it plain on tablets, so he may run who reads it."

He thought about that for a while. What did that mean for them? Was writing down their goals and vision really the thing they'd been missing this whole time? Could something so simple, so practical, so fundamental be the key to changing their business around?

He looked out the window and saw Ricki setting up the bikes for them. He put the Bible back and headed out to meet his wife.

Hope is not a strategy.

—Rick Page

ACTION STEP

Stop winging it—get your strategy on paper. Download or print your one-page Accelerate business plan template by scanning the following QR code or visiting accelerate playbook.com. Set aside dedicated time this week to complete each section: your business's goals, game plan, gaps, and go plan. Keep your plan visible and refer to it as your North Star for decision-making. Schedule a thirty-minute review every month to update your plan as your business grows and changes. If you have different divisions for your company, complete a one-page plan for each one. Completing your one-page plan will help you focus on what matters most, communicate your vision to you and your team, and ensure everyone is aligned and moving in the same direction.

CHAPTER 7

THE DIAGNOSTIC DEEP DIVE
Uncovering Hidden Gaps

When they got to the trail, Anthony adjusted the seat of the mountain bike, gearing up to ride. During his NFL days, he'd loved going on long bike rides during his off-season, and sitting on this bike brought him right back to the feeling of speeding down the neighborhood bike path, blasting his favorite playlist and spending hours feeling like he was flying. He pushed off and attempted to get his feet off the ground, but instead of coasting forward, the bike wobbled beneath him and veered toward the edge of the trail, forcing him to stop and plant his feet on the ground.

"Hold on. Something's not right here," Anthony said, dismounting. He put the kickstand down and walked around the bike, inspecting it.

"Yeah, look here," he said, grabbing the handlebars. "When I turn the handlebars like this," he held the handlebars straight, "the wheel still goes a little to the right. The alignment is off," he said, pointing to the wheels.

Ricki came over to inspect. "Yeah, you're right," she said. "And look back here. It looks like the frame is bent a little." She pointed to the back of the bike.

Ricki could see a look of disappointment cross her husband's face, and she immediately went into "fix it" mode. "Now that you know about the alignment, could you ride it in a way that compensates for it? Like try and keep the handlebars a little off center?" she asked with a shrug.

Anthony got back on the bike, picked his feet off the ground, and tried again to steady the bike, focusing on keeping the handlebars at an unnatural angle in order to keep his balance. It didn't work.

"Nope," he said finally, getting off the bike and walking it. They walked their bikes for a while until they reached the crest of a hill. They parked their bikes under a sprawling oak tree near the shore and made their way to a coffee truck parked nearby. Anthony ordered two coffees, and they carried their steaming cups to a wooden bench beneath the tree.

Sitting side by side, they took in the view for a moment, letting the peaceful sound of the waves settle over them.

"You know, as we were walking up here, I was thinking about the bike," said Anthony. "And that even though I'm perfectly capable of riding a bike, there's nothing I can do about that if the structure of the bike is broken." He sipped his coffee and looked over at Ricki, who was waiting for him to continue.

"We can do our best in our business and know all the steps, but if the systems aren't right, if we aren't aligned, we're never going to get anywhere," he said thoughtfully.

Ricki considered this for a moment. "That's a great point. It was like no matter how hard you worked to stay balanced, the bike just wasn't going to cooperate. And, if we want to go really deep with this bike metaphor . . ." she smiled and went on. "We could look at the reasons the bike is bent and misaligned in the first place."

Anthony shifted his body toward her. "Go on," he said, remembering how much he loved watching her think.

"Maybe it got left out in the rain. Maybe someone ran it over with a truck. Maybe it was neglected or ignored for a long time. Maybe someone used the heck out of it but didn't worry about bike maintenance," she said slowly.

"Or maybe it hit a few bumps in the road and caused some damage that nobody saw until now, when we looked at it closely," Anthony added.

"So maybe it's not just about the fact that the bike is unrideable now, it's about all the little things that led up to it being like that," Ricki said. "It's the same with our business. Or even with us," she added, turning serious. "We didn't just wake up with a broken business. We're noticing it now because we can't move forward no matter how hard we try. It's neglect, on both of our parts, or unresolved issues that have built up. So even if we took that ol' thing to a bike shop and they fixed the frame and the alignment, we'd still need to learn how to take better care of the bike so it doesn't happen again."

"We can think of this trip as preventative maintenance," Anthony agreed. "So when we work on things like communicating better, or analyzing our strengths and weaknesses, or just taking time to assess what we have, what's working, what's not, what needs to be fine-tuned, we're keeping the frame of our business strong and aligned."

"Coach would be so proud of us," Ricki laughed, holding up her coffee cup to toast Anthony's.

"Agreed. Now, let's finish this coffee and head back. I'm ready to start making some moves," Anthony replied.

As they sat there, sipping their drinks, the sun climbing higher in the sky, both felt a sense of renewal. They weren't just tackling a bike ride, they were learning how to tackle life together, one wobbly pedal stroke at a time.

‖‖‖‖‖‖‖

The scent of sizzling meat wafted through the air as Anthony and Ricki walked their bikes up the gravel path to the bed and breakfast. The familiar screech of the screen door greeted them, followed by the low rumble of Coach's voice from the side yard.

Anthony spotted him first, standing by a large grill with a pair of tongs in one hand and a beer in the other. He waved them over.

"Well, look who's back!" Coach called, flipping a set of burgers with a practiced flick of his wrist. "How was the ride?"

"Great," Anthony replied, parking his bike. "Eventually."

Coach raised an eyebrow, amused, but didn't press. Ricki smiled knowingly and made her way toward the house.

"I'm going to see what goodies Edna has inside," she said. "I'll leave you two to . . . grill things."

Anthony chuckled as she disappeared through the door, then turned back to Coach. He reached for a bottle of water from the nearby cooler and leaned against the railing of the deck.

Coach gestured toward the grill with his tongs. "I was thinking about our conversation earlier, about analyzing, and I had a realization: Being on the grill is a lot like analyzing, you know. If you don't pay attention, don't check the temperature, don't adjust the heat, you'll end up with burnt burgers and a disappointed crowd. I don't cook just for me—I need to prepare food for the masses."

Anthony laughed. "I think I can handle burgers. Analyzing my marriage and my business, though? That's a whole different story."

Coach turned, his expression more serious now. "Is it, though? Think about it. Just like with this grill, you've got to check in regularly with your partner. If something's off, too hot, too cold, out of balance, you address it. Otherwise, things start to burn."

Anthony nodded, taking a long sip of water. "Makes sense. But it's hard to admit when something's not working. Especially when you feel like you should be able to handle it."

Coach's eyes softened. "Anthony, let me tell you something I've learned the hard way. Marriage isn't about handling everything yourself. It's about partnership. Recognizing your strengths, leaning on each other when you need to, and being honest about what you need to work on. The same principles that make a great team on the field make a great team at home."

Anthony leaned on the railing, considering this. "I guess I've been so focused on being the 'strong one' that I haven't thought about what Ricki needs from me. Or what I need from her."

Coach nodded. "That's the key, communication. And not just the surface-level stuff. You've got to analyze the patterns. What's working in your marriage? What's not? What needs to change? And you have to be willing to adjust."

Anthony smirked. "You sound like you're still coaching."

Coach laughed, flipping a burger. "Once a coach, always a coach. But trust me, this is one playbook worth studying."

Inside, Ricki found Edna in the kitchen, slicing fresh tomatoes and arranging them on a platter.

"Need any help?" Ricki offered.

Edna smiled, handing her a bunch of basil. "You can tear this up for the salad if you'd like. And maybe join me out on the porch. It's too nice a day to stay cooped up in here."

The two women carried the salad fixings outside and settled into the wicker chairs on the front porch. Edna poured them each a glass of lemonade from a tray already set up on the small table between them.

"So," Edna began, her tone gentle, "how are things going with you and Anthony? Not just the business—everything."

Ricki, normally very guarded, felt unusually comfortable and hesitated for a moment before answering. "We're figuring it out. Today was a good step, I think. But it's hard sometimes. Balancing everything. Communicating. Knowing when to step back and when to push forward."

Edna nodded, her expression empathetic. "It is hard. And anyone who tells you otherwise isn't being honest. But you know what makes it easier?"

"What's that?" Ricki asked, sipping her lemonade.

"Checking in with *yourself* as much as you check in with him," Edna said. "I've learned that if I don't take the time to reflect on what I need, what I'm feeling, it's impossible to show up fully for Stanley or for our guests. It's like Coach always says: 'Every great journey begins by understanding what you're carrying with you.' That applies to marriage, too. You've got to know what baggage you're bringing into it, good and bad."

Ricki tore a basil leaf in half thoughtfully. "That's true. I think sometimes I focus so much on what Anthony needs, or on the business, that I forget to ask myself what I need. What baggage am I carrying? My family went through a lot before I even met Anthony."

Edna smiled. "You're not alone in that. It's easy to lose yourself in the busyness of life. But when you take the time to reflect, to understand your own patterns and triggers, you'll find it so much easier to navigate the tough moments together."

Ricki looked out toward the yard, where Anthony and Coach were laughing about something by the grill.

"You know," Ricki said, turning back to Edna, "I think this trip was exactly what we needed. Not just for the business, but for us. I feel lighter already."

Edna raised her glass with a knowing smile. "To new beginnings, and better playbooks."

Ricki clinked her glass against Edna's, a small but hopeful smile spreading across her face.

Just then, the familiar Mercedes came crunching up the driveway. The car came to a stop, but David and Darla didn't get out. Instead, they stayed seated, clearly in the middle of a heated conversation. Ricki pretended to focus on her drink, but couldn't help looking at the drama happening right in front of them. Darla noticed Ricki watching them and mumbled something, and then David looked too. They immediately got out of the car, a big (and fake) smile plastered on David's face. He sauntered up to the porch. Darla went straight inside and up the stairs.

Everyone looked at David expectantly. He sighed and sat down on the porch swing. "It's nothing, really. A little trouble in paradise—but hey, that's life, right?" he said, trying to sound casual. Anthony and Coach slowly moved from the grill up to the porch.

"What's going on? Seemed a little tense," Edna asked.

"Things have been a little rough lately," David admitted. "I got in a big fight with my dad before we left. My whole life he's been prepping me to take over the family business. My family owns a manufacturing company, and it's always been his dream for me to take it over. He's going to retire in a few years, and so he keeps pressing me to get more involved."

"Are you not interested in manufacturing?" Edna asked.

"It's not that. I actually love it. I've been surrounded by it my whole life, and I always pictured myself in my dad's big corner office, overseeing everything."

"So what's the problem?"

"He always said things like, 'Son, one day all of this will be yours,' or 'David, I am so confident that you will be able to run this entire thing even better than I have . . ." He trailed off.

Everyone on the porch looked at him, confused. *What's the problem?* Anthony thought to himself.

"And that's great and everything," David continued, "but when he's talking about me getting more involved, he's talking about starting at entry level. He's talking about me being an assembly line worker or a filling machine operator. I had this whole list of changes we can make to the company, to make it more modern and efficient. Worked hard on that list too. And he didn't even want to hear it." David sounded distraught.

Ricki shot a glance at Anthony. Was she missing something? Here was this kid, handsome, apparently rich, and being handed the family's very successful business. What was the problem?

"He said I had to 'get to know the business from the bottom up,'" David said, rolling his eyes and using air quotes. "He said I need to know every aspect of the business so that I know how each department works with the next. He says it will help me hire better." David's voice was almost turning into a whine, and Ricki half expected him to stomp his feet like a toddler.

When everyone was still looking at him, waiting for the big problem, he threw his hands up, exasperated.

"He wants me to work in the *warehouse*!" he almost yelled. "He wants me to do *X* and *Y* and spend years, *years*, working in all of these different positions. And most of that time I won't even get to make big decisions and I'll be making like, nothing."

The whole porch was silent. *Was this kid for real?* Anthony thought. *He's here crying because Daddy told him he has to work his way up within the company? That he's basically promised a six-figure salary before he's thirty if he just works for it?* Anthony could tell everyone on the porch was thinking the same thing, but nobody was going to call him out on it.

Except Coach.

"So let me get this right," Coach said, shifting his weight from one foot to the next. "Your dad is the CEO of this business, and he's built it from the ground up. This was his idea, that he turned into a reality. It's his blood, sweat, and tears that have made this business a wild success. And you've grown up around it, you probably have known some of the people who work for him since you were in diapers. Am I getting this right?"

David nodded.

"And you've expressed interest in taking over when the time comes. You've already pictured yourself in that fancy office, wearing that fancy custom suit, driving that fancy luxury car. You've already envisioned yourself bringing home the big bucks, buying a big ol' fancy house for that fiancée of yours, and carrying out your dad's legacy," Coach continued. David nodded, excited that someone was finally hearing him, understanding him.

"And he has the *audacity*, the pure audacity, to insist you start at the ground floor. That you immerse yourself in every aspect of the business so that you know it like the back of your hand. He is insisting that you get your hands dirty, that you become intimately familiar with the way each part of the business works so that you have a solid understanding of how it all works. So that you have the knowledge you need to be a good leader. So that you have the experience you need to continue running this business, so that you have the resources required to expand and build a legacy," Coach said, his eyes not moving from David's. As Coach talked, David's smile fell.

This was not how he thought this conversation was going to go, thought Ricki.

David stammered a little bit. "Well, yeah, I mean . . . no. It's complicated. I know the business. I grew up around it. I got my degree, and he said that once I graduated it would be time to start getting more involved. I always thought that meant becoming some figurehead, some sort of decision-maker."

"That's not how it works, son," Coach said gently. "Your dad didn't just appear at the top. He worked his way to get there. He put in the hours, the time, the commitment. You ever play video games? You don't get to start at level ten. You start at level one and get all the stars and coins and bananas you need to level up."

I think he's combining a few different video games, Anthony thought to himself, but let it go.

"That big fight we got in right before we left?" said David. "He urged us to stay and talk it out, but I couldn't listen to him anymore. So we drove and drove and ended up here. We just needed a place to get away so we could think. Maybe come up with a new plan? Maybe start our own business."

"A new plan that will have you starting out at level ten?" Coach asked. David thought it over, and shrugged.

"Listen, I know you're only supposed to be here for tonight, and I don't usually do this, but I think you should stay one more night," Coach said. "Stay a little longer, let us help you work this out."

"But that's the thing! I don't need help. I don't need advice—no offense—from people who don't know how a real business works," David snapped.

Anthony and Ricki tensed, their eyes shooting over to Coach to get his reaction. He didn't give one.

"So what's her deal?" Coach asked, jutting his thumb toward the house.

"Darla? Oh, she's just a little . . . confused. Frustrated. Our parents have known each other for a long time, and we've been friends since middle school. The plan was for us to graduate, Dad would hand over the business like he said, and we'd get married. But now that it's looking like it's going to be a while before the business is actually mine, she feels . . ." David trailed off, not knowing how to finish.

Everyone on the porch looked at each other with the same knowing glance. *She thought he was going to walk right into Daddy's office and start getting that paycheck. And now that he's not . . .* Ricki thought. *Poor kid*, she added, looking over at David.

"David. Will you consider staying tonight and tomorrow?" asked Coach. "Explore the Vineyard, try some of the great food, walk by the water, take some time for just the two of you. And then let me try and help. I may just be an old guy who runs a bed and breakfast," he said, winking at Ricki and Anthony, "but I know a thing or two about hard work. Will you listen?"

David ran his fingers through his hair just as the screen door screeched open and Darla walked out onto the porch. "Ready?" she asked, looking only at David. He looked apologetically at everyone on the porch and stood up. "We're going out for a bit. We will be back later." He offered a half smile and followed his fiancée to the car. Everyone on the porch was silent as they watched the sleek luxury car disappear from sight.

"Think you'll be able to get to them, Coach?" Ricki asked.

Coach grinned confidently. "I'm always up for a challenge."

You cannot change what you are unaware of.

—T. D. Jakes, *Disruptive Thinking*

ACTION STEP

Complete the Business Audit* to assess key areas of your business, such as finances, operations, marketing, customer service, and team performance.

Identify Strengths and Gaps: Review your audit results and highlight at least one area where your business is performing well and one area that needs improvement or immediate attention.

Set a Measurable Improvement Goal: Choose the most critical area for improvement. Write down a specific, measurable goal for this area (e.g., "Increase customer retention by

* You can access the Business Audit at accelerateplaybook.com.

10% in the next quarter" or "Reduce order processing errors by 50% in thirty days").

Develop and Implement an Action Step: List one concrete action you will take this week to start addressing your chosen improvement area. Assign responsibility if you have a team, and set a deadline.

Schedule a Follow-Up Review: Mark your calendar for a thirty-day check-in to review your progress, adjust your action plan if needed, and celebrate any wins.

Why this works: Regularly analyzing your business and taking targeted action leads to continuous improvement, better decision-making, and greater long-term success. By making this a habit, you position your business to adapt, grow, and outperform the competition.

CHAPTER 8

STRATEGIC ORDER
Transforming Chaos into Control

Ricki, a natural early riser, was sitting up against the window the next morning at the small writing desk, reflecting on her notes from the previous day. A commotion from outside caught her attention, and she peered out the window down to the gravel driveway below. She noticed David and Darla's Mercedes was back, which meant they'd gotten home late the night before, after everyone had retired from the firepit and gone to bed. The sound of Nate's frustrated groan echoed up to Ricki's window as he rifled through the back of his van, scattering random supplies like a tornado. "I swear it was right here!"

Clara stood nearby, arms crossed, trying to stay patient. "We're going to miss the market if we don't leave soon," she said, her tone a mix of exasperation and defeat. "I still don't understand why we had to leave in such a hurry. We could have given ourselves an extra day and packed up like normal human beings. But you insisted we just throw in everything and hit the road, and now we can't find anything!" Clara said, practically vibrating with impatience.

Nate ignored her, sorting through suitcases and a bin marked "coffee supplies." He stepped over an espresso machine, a mini fridge, and a plastic sleeve of paper coffee cups to dig deeper into the van.

"And all of this stuff!" she added, raising her voice and leaning into the van. "We don't even have a truck yet, but we have an espresso machine and a mini fridge and a box full of vanilla syrup!"

Ricki shook her head, bemused, as Nate pulled out a plastic container only to pop it open and find it was full of bags of coffee. "Clara, I know it's here somewhere!" he called out, his voice tinged with equal parts determination and desperation.

Ricki couldn't help but chuckle. The scene was both chaotic and oddly relatable. She had been in their shoes before, scrambling at the last minute, searching for something lost in the abyss of disorganization. It was a reminder of how quickly things could spiral when there wasn't a plan in place.

As she watched the scene unfold, she jotted down a quick note to herself: "Organization isn't just about neatness, it brings efficiency. It's about making life easier so you can enjoy the things you care about. It's about peace."

Ricki took a shower and got dressed. Once Anthony was also showered and dressed, the two of them made their way downstairs to the kitchen, following the unmistakable smell of bacon.

"Morning, you two!" Coach said with a smile.

For some reason, his warm welcome made Ricki think about something her grandma used to say. *There are two types of people in this world. "Here I am" people and "There you are" people. "Here I am" people walk into a room and want you to know that they've arrived. "There you are" people walk into a room and want you to know that you are seen.*

Coach was definitely a *there you are* type of person, and Ricki was thankful for that. Even over the clinking and chatting and sizzling going on in the kitchen, Ricki could still hear Nate and Clara's heated discussion outside in the front. Ricki noticed when Edna heard it too. Without a word, she assigned Coach to bacon duty and walked out of the kitchen and onto the front porch.

"Do you two need some help?" Edna asked, in a tone that reminded Ricki of her mother's serious and scolding voice. Thanks to the open window in the kitchen, everyone at the table sat quietly to hear the conversation happening outside.

"We need to leave for the market in fifteen minutes," Clara explained. "We're meeting with an old friend of my dad's. He's interested in investing in our coffee truck, and we plan to meet him there at eight. But my phone is dead, and we only have one charger, and we can't find it. All the information about where we're meeting and some documents I made for the meeting are on my phone, and I can't get to it," Clara complained, her sentences running together.

Ricki could hear the frustration and panic in Clara's voice. Nate was still rifling through their van, his movements becoming more frantic by the second. But Edna, ever the composed one, stayed calm.

"You know, this—" Edna started, her voice quiet but firm, "this is a perfect example of why organization is so important, not just for your personal life, but for your business too." She paused for a moment, making sure they were listening.

Clara stopped for a moment, caught by Edna's observation. Nate, still flustered, looked up, his face a mix of embarrassment and frustration.

"Disorganization," Edna continued, "often speaks to something much deeper. It tells me that you're not prepared, that you're reactive rather than proactive. It shows a lack of planning, and, frankly, it tells me you might not be taking your business, or your future, seriously. You want a coffee truck, right? That's an investment, and you have to treat it like one. If you can't organize your day-to-day life, how are you going to manage the big stuff? Your finances? Your marketing? Your operations? Your inventory?"

She didn't wait for them to respond. "Organization isn't just about keeping things neat. It's about creating systems so you can focus on what matters. When you don't have systems, when everything is in disarray, you end up wasting time, like this." She gestured toward the van, which looked like a small disaster zone. "You're wasting time looking for something that should already have a place. Time you don't have, especially when you've got an important meeting scheduled."

Clara shifted uncomfortably, clearly processing Edna's words. Nate stayed quiet, but he was listening intently.

Edna's voice softened a bit. "You've got to take the time to get organized. It doesn't happen overnight. You have to be disciplined. When you're organized, you're giving yourself more freedom to think clearly, to focus, to move forward. And it doesn't just help you in life—it's going to make your business run smoother too. I promise you, it's the foundation of success."

Clara bit her lip, glancing over at Nate, who was still standing next to the van. Edna's eyes softened with a knowing smile.

"Now, I'm going to help you out so you don't miss your meeting," Edna said warmly. She reached into the pocket of her apron and pulled out a phone charger, handing it to Clara. "Take this— you're going to need it."

Ricki watched from the kitchen, surprised at how gracefully Edna had stepped in, and how much wisdom she was imparting without even a hint of judgment.

"As soon as you get back," Edna added, turning to head inside, "we're going to organize that van. You'll have to face this mess head-on. You can't run away from it. I'll be waiting. We'll do it together."

Clara's eyes lit up as she accepted the charger. "Thanks, Edna. Really."

Nate, looking both relieved and humbled, gave Edna a nod of gratitude. "We'll clean it up. I promise."

Edna, satisfied, nodded firmly. "I'm holding you to that."

She disappeared back into the house, leaving Nate and Clara to power-walk to their van and hit the road.

Ricki felt a quiet sense of admiration for Edna. Her calm, practical approach had not only solved the immediate problem but had set the stage for something bigger: the realization that organization was more than just a tool—it was a way of life, one that could shape their business, their future, and their peace of mind.

As they all settled back into the kitchen, their conversation came to a halt when they heard raised voices coming from upstairs. It was David and Darla, clearly having another argument. Anthony shot Ricki a glance that said, *None of my business*, and went back to his breakfast. The sound of a door opening upstairs was followed by quickly moving feet coming down the stairs. It was clear they were heading outside, but the stares of everyone in the kitchen stopped them in their tracks. Darla continued out to the porch while David plastered on that smile again and transformed into Mr. Charming.

"We're staying another night. I thought about what you said, and I'm open to hearing more. Can't promise I'll change my mind, but we've got to do something different here. She's not thrilled," he said, tilting his head toward the front porch. "But she agreed to one extra night. Maybe you can help us figure out a new business plan."

"Glad to hear it, David," Coach said, holding his coffee mug up like he was giving a toast.

|||||||||||

A few hours later, Nate and Clara's van came crunching up the gravel driveway. Anthony and Coach were in the middle of football talk, and Edna and Ricki were sharing stories about what it was like being married to someone who was married to football.

"How'd the meeting go?" Coach asked.

Clara smiled and returned the charger to Edna. "Great—once we got the phone charged and figured out where we were going. That farmer's market up there is cute, you guys should check it out while you're here," Clara said to Anthony and Ricki, plopping down on the porch.

"Meeting went great," Nate said, redirecting the conversation back to Coach's question. "He's interested in our idea, and our visions for the truck align in a lot of ways. He posed some questions we need to think about," Nate said, holding up a crumpled piece of paper, "so we're going to dive into that tonight!"

"*After* we organize the van," Edna said pointedly to Nate.

Ricki couldn't tell, but Nate's face almost looked disappointed, like he thought maybe she'd forget. He recovered quickly and put on a smile. "Right, after we organize the van."

Edna slapped her knees and stood up. "Right, then let's get to it!"

"Now?" Clara asked.

"What better time than the present?" Edna replied with a cheerful smile, heading toward the van. Clara and Nate gave each other a resigned look and followed closely behind. Ricki stood to go inside, but Coach's voice stopped her.

"You may want to stay for this," he said quietly, gesturing at Edna as she slid open the van door and put her hands on her hips. Ricki sat back down.

"The first step to organizing is figuring out what you've got and what you actually need," Edna said with authority. "Let's pull everything out and take stock. Here's the rule: If you haven't used it in the past month or you don't have a specific plan to use it soon, it goes in storage or gets donated. Sound fair?"

Nate and Clara nodded, and the three of them got to work. Ricki wondered if they were embarrassed, having a stranger root through all of their junk. But as she watched them sort, she decided that sometimes you have to swallow your pride, let someone else in, and trust the process.

After a while, Clara stood back with her hands on her hips. "This makes so much sense," she said. "I didn't realize how much time we waste just digging around for stuff."

"Now, that's much better," Edna said with a proud smile, admiring their handiwork. "How you do anything is how you do everything," she said confidently. Ricki's ears perked up.

"What'd you say, Edna?" Ricki called from the porch. Edna turned around and faced her.

"How you do anything is how you do everything," she repeated with a confident nod, clearly proud of the final result.

Ricki thought about her childhood, how she'd always felt this push to be the best. She was the one who would do a group project all on her own because she couldn't trust her classmates to do it right. In college, she said no to parties and social activities so she could study; on the soccer field, she got there earlier, stayed later, and worked until she was exhausted. And now, with her business, she felt like she was always working the hardest and worrying the most, not leaving room for anyone else to come take the load off. *How you do anything is how you do everything*, she thought to herself.

"You know, this feels a lot like what Coach was talking about yesterday. It's not just about fixing the mess, it's about . . . what was the word he used?" Nate stopped to think for a second. "Recalibrating. Taking a step back, figuring out what's working and what's not, and coming up with a plan to move forward."

Edna smiled. "Exactly. And this wasn't just about making sure you have a clean, organized van to drive around in. It's a metaphor for running a successful business. Running a successful business is kind of like planning an epic road trip. Every so often, you have to stop, take stock of where you are, and make adjustments. If you don't, you'll just keep running into the same problems."

Anthony moved up to the front porch and stood next to Ricki. "It's kind of like our business. We've been so focused on just *doing the work* that we haven't taken the time to organize our processes, or even decide who's responsible for what. No wonder we're always scrambling."

Ricki looked up at him and smiled. "I was thinking the same thing. We've been treating our business like their van, just throwing things in wherever they fit and hoping it works."

"When you're disorganized, you're constantly in reaction mode," Edna added. "But when you've got a plan, you can be proactive. You can anticipate challenges and handle them without falling apart. If you want to be busy, stay unorganized, if you want to be productive, get organized. Some business leaders are productive, while most business leaders are busy."

Ricki thought for a second and looked back up at Anthony. "That's deep. Maybe it's time to pull everything out, just like they did. Figure out what we're carrying, what we actually need, and how to organize it so we're not tripping over ourselves all the time."

The whole porch was quiet for a while until Ricki said, "It feels overwhelming. There's so much to fix I don't even know where to start."

Edna patted her knee. "Here's the thing, Ricki: You don't have to fix everything at once. Big changes happen in small, deliberate steps. Let's break it down. First things first: Have you and Anthony ever mapped out your audacious goals? That's the foundation of any successful venture. What is the end goal?"

There's that phrase again, Anthony thought. *An audacious goal.* Anthony and Ricki looked at each other. They both started to speak, but Anthony gestured for Ricki to answer.

"Not really," Ricki admitted. "We've talked about them, but nothing's written down. We've just been—"

"Winging it," Anthony said, glancing sheepishly over at Coach as he remembered how they'd had to make the same admission earlier in the week.

Edna nodded. "That's step one, then. Sit down together and write out your long-term goals. What do you want your business to look like a year from now? Five years? Once you've got the big picture, you can work backward to figure out what needs to happen next."

Ricki tilted her head, intrigued. "Okay, so start with the goals. What's next?"

"Uh uh," Coach said, shaking his head and letting out a soft chuckle. "No jumping ahead. Write down your goals first, and then we move ahead. I understand that you like to see the whole picture, Ricki, but sometimes that distracts you from doing the one small step that is in front of you. Goals first. Where are you going? What is your final destination?" He raised an eyebrow as if to challenge her.

Ricki glanced at Anthony, and he shrugged. "Okay, we'll write down our goals," Ricki said confidently. Then the porch was silent again. Ricki started looking around and realized everyone was looking at her.

"Oh! Now?" she asked.

Edna and Coach didn't answer, just smiled at her like parents who were watching their child answer her own question. Anthony opened up the screen door for her, and Ricki walked inside. As the door closed behind her, she heard Coach and Edna's quiet voices. She couldn't make out most of what they were saying, but as she started up the stairs she heard, "They're gonna be fine," in Coach's unmistakable baritone. Before they could get all the way up the stairs, Edna called from the porch. "Look in the desk drawer. There's a page in there I think you'll find useful."

When they got up to the room, Ricki went right to the desk and opened the drawer. Inside she saw a crisp white sheet of paper split into four different sections:

A few hours later, Ricki and Anthony came back downstairs and followed the clinks and clatters of movement in the kitchen. Edna was staring out the window and turned when she heard them come in.

"How'd it go?" she asked, putting the big mixing bowl she was holding down on the counter and pulling up a chair.

Ricki slid the sheet of paper across the table wordlessly and watched as Edna read over their work.

ACCELERATE

COMPANY GOAL: _____

GOALS
WHAT **BIG** RESULTS?

1. Increase revenue by 2.5 million

2. 25 new clients

3. Create clear SOP

What does success look like
for your Company?

GAME PLAN
WHAT **BIG** MOVES?

1. Add a new personal assistant

2. Create more client events

3. Streamline operations

What plays do you need to run
by End of Year?

ONE-PAGE PLAN

GAPS
WHAT **BIG** OBSTACLES ?

1. Unorganized

2. Lack structure

3. Stabilize financials

What is getting in the way of you and your team's success,
e.g., unorganized, inability to measure, understaffed?

GO! GO! GO!
WHAT **BIG** TIMELINES?

1. Create hiring plan

2. Begin Formalizing all processes

3. Schedule off-season for next year

What next step are you committed
to taking in next 7 days?

WORKSHEET

WWW.ACCELERATEPLAYBOOK.COM

"Good work, guys. It looks like you put a lot of thought into this. I know this seems like a little step, but it's the discipline to write it down that makes the difference," Edna said, sliding the paper back.

"This is great. It really has me charged up about what we will be able to do when we get home. I'm going to put this in my suitcase," Ricki said, standing up from the table, but stopped when she heard Edna speak.

"One suggestion," she said, holding up a finger. "Don't tuck it away. Put it out on your desk in the room so you can see it every day for the rest of your trip. When you get home, make sure it's your North Star guiding your every step. Maybe tape it to the bathroom mirror so you can look at it when you're getting ready in the morning and each night."

"Great idea!" Ricki said, and almost skipped out of the kitchen and up the stairs. Edna stood up and resumed her mixing. When Ricki came back down, Anthony noticed an excited glow in her eyes. A hunger, a determination he hadn't seen in a while.

She clapped her hands together and said, "Okay! Now what?" looking eagerly at Edna.

Edna smiled a knowing smile and stopped mixing. "You want to do this now?" she asked.

"What better time than the present?" Ricki smiled, mirroring Edna's words from earlier. Edna smiled too. "Okay, let me finish these blueberry muffins and I'll meet you on the porch," she said.

Ricki and Anthony stood up, pushed their chairs in, and walked out to the porch.

"So now it's about getting organized," Edna said a minute later, coming through the front door in her infamous cat apron. "Organization for you two is not going to be about putting things in bins or keeping your workspace and living space clean. It seems like you've got that part covered. *You haven't seen our garage*, Anthony thought to himself. "Organization for you two is going to look more like being intentional about who's doing what, how and when you're going to communicate, and how you're going to track your success."

They looked at Edna quietly, waiting for her to go on.

"Coach, honey, can you come here for a bit? I think you're going to want to be part of this conversation," she called out toward the garden. Coach put his gardening tools down, wiped his dirty hands on his jeans, and joined the group on the porch.

"I was just telling Ricki and Anthony that for them, being organized is not going to be about having a tidy workspace or knowing when to get rid of stuff that is holding them down. Organization for them is going to look a little different, and I thought you'd have a few things to say about that," Edna explained.

A smile spread across Coach's face, and he cleared his throat. "You know, I love this stuff," Coach said, rubbing his hands together like he was preparing a team for a big play. "First, you need to know your end zone. What's the goal? Write it down, make it clear."

"They just did that," Edna said, explaining how they'd just spent a good amount of time on their one-page plan.

"Well, great! Now that you have the big picture, you've got to break it down into plays: small, actionable steps that'll get you there. And just like on the field, everyone needs to know their position. If you're both trying to play quarterback, you're gonna trip over each other. It can be so easy to get caught up in the day-to-day grind that you forget to really define who does what. Who's taking charge of what part of this business, and who's going to own the rest?"

Anthony nodded, his gaze softening. "Right. We've been working together, but sometimes it feels like we're doing everything together, and no one's really leading the way. We've got to split it up so we're both playing to our strengths. So for us, it's like one person needs to be the quarterback, lay out the plan, keep us aligned. The other is the workhorse, the one executing, making sure the day-to-day operations are running smoothly. When we both try to be the decision-maker or the 'boss'"—here he used air quotes—"at the same time, nothing gets done."

"It's like when we were on the field, if we both tried to run the same play, it would get messy," Coach added. "You need to be strategic, play to your strengths, and divide the work so it doesn't all fall on one person. You've got the vision, Ricki. You've got the strategy. And you've got the drive, Anthony. Focus on that."

Ricki leaned back, the weight of the conversation settling in. "We've been so focused on surviving, we forgot about playing to win. It's time to redefine the roles and make sure we're both empowered in the process."

"Exactly," Coach said, giving her an encouraging smile. "You've got to play the long game, break down the steps, and trust each other. Most importantly, don't just show up on the field. *Own it.*"

A beeping sound came from inside the house, and Edna stood up quickly. "The muffins are ready!" she exclaimed, getting up from her rocking chair to go inside. Ricki shivered as she noticed the sun was setting and the shady porch was feeling a little chilly.

"So . . . *I'm* the quarterback?" Ricki teased, nudging Anthony with her elbow. His eyes widened, and then he said, "The smartest, most beautiful quarterback I've ever seen."

Just then, David and Darla came out onto the porch. "Ah! There they are," said Coach, meeting the hesitant couple with a smile.

"Ricki, Anthony, if you'll excuse us, we're going on a little field trip. Should be back before it gets dark," Coach said, leading the way down the porch followed by David and Darla.

Ricki watched as they all piled in Edna's car and disappeared down the driveway.

‖‖‖‖‖‖‖‖‖

About twenty minutes later, the car pulled into a wide-open parking lot.

"Where are we?" David asked.

"You'll see," Coach answered as he put his car in park and walked toward the front door of a small building. The windows were hand-painted with colorful images of coffee beans and steaming coffee mugs, and the sign above the door said: "Beanies Small Coffee Roastery."

"Coffee? Now?" David asked. Coach looked back at him, winked, and held the door open for them. The place looked closed, but a short, stocky man in a blue apron was busy behind the counter.

"Coach! So good to see you!" he said, coming forward and shaking Coach's hand.

"Marco, thanks for doing this last minute. These are some new friends of mine, David and Darla."

"Nice to meet you. If I know anything about Coach, I'm guessing you have no idea why you're here?" Marco asked, raising an eyebrow. David shook his head. "That sounds like Coach to me. So, what are we learning today, Coach? The art of coffee bean roasting?"

"Not quite," said Coach. "These two are about to start a new, exciting chapter in their lives. They're on the brink of starting a new career, but are a little unclear on the importance of understanding, *really understanding*, every aspect of their business. They've got their eyes set on the head honcho position," Coach said, patting David on the back. "But he doesn't quite have a clear plan or path on how to get there. I thought I could bring him here to show him how important it is to really know every aspect of a business." Coach's eyes moved in such a way that Marco could hear what Coach wasn't saying and read between the lines.

"Love it! Okay, well, follow me. A good cup of coffee starts with beans." Marco walked toward the back wall, which was lined with burlap sacks of coffee beans. He dipped his hand into a barrel full of beans and let them cascade out of his fingers. "So much potential in these little guys." He moved toward the roasting area, where he explained the logistics and details involved in turning the beans from a pale green to a dark brown. He explained the careful balance of time and temperature, and how it could take employees weeks to learn how to manage both.

"There's no rushing in this process. If you try to skip ahead, you either end up burning the beans or losing the flavor," Marco explained.

"So it's about patience?" Coach asked. "And doing it the right way? *In order*?" Coach emphasized the last part.

Marco nodded and moved them to the brewing station. He explained that during the day the baristas were here, busy measuring, grinding, and brewing the beans with precision. At this step, every detail mattered: water temperature, grind size, even how they poured. "Everyone here needs to have a deep understanding of all of these things because when we get busy, we need all hands on deck. We need everyone to know everything about all of it. That's what makes us such a strong and efficient team," Marco said proudly.

They moved through the roastery, listening to Marco passionately explain bean origin and quality, moisture content, bean size, and roast levels. When Coach noticed David's eyes start to glaze over, he gave Marco a subtle sign that let him know they were ready to go. Marco put a burlap sack of beans in David and Darla's hands as a gift. "Remember, a great leader doesn't just enjoy the rewards—they respect the work that goes into them," Marco said, holding the roastery door open for them. They said their goodbyes and got back into the car.

Everyone was quiet for a moment, and Coach was surprised to hear Darla's voice come from the backseat: "Leadership isn't just about making decisions from the top. You have to know the roots of your business."

Coach and David shot each other a look, and Coach turned around to face her. "Exactly. I know you guys have this audacious goal for David to be CEO and be successful and make a lot of money and continue his father's legacy, but all of that is like a steaming hot cup of coffee back there. There are steps you have to follow. You can't skip steps. And you can't compare your bag of beans to someone else's artisanal coffee. There's a process. Right now, you guys are trying to find a way to skip the roasting and the water temperature regulation and the waiting and the grinding and skip right to the part where you drink the coffee. That's not how it works, and that's all your dad has been trying to say."

Coach started the car and pulled out of the parking lot, watching Beanies fade away in his rearview mirror.

When they got back to the house, Nate, Clara, Ricki, Anthony, and Edna were seated around the firepit. Coach, David, and Darla joined them. Ricki saw Coach give Edna a wink, and she responded with a single nod.

"What do you think they talked about?" Anthony whispered to Ricki as David and Darla explained to the others why they were holding a bag of beans.

"I don't know," Ricki answered, but she could tell Coach had worked his magic. Darla looked more relaxed, and David had this sense of excitement in his voice. It wasn't just a bag of coffee beans they were holding, but an understanding, a lesson that had settled deep and could possibly change the trajectory of their lives.

Clutter is postponed decisions.

—Barbara Hemphill

ACTION STEP

Download and complete the "What's in Your Hands?" Resource Inventory Checklist by scanning the following QR code. Take stock of every resource you already have: products, people, systems, partnerships, and technology. For each resource, honestly assess: Are you using it? How valuable is it—high, medium, or low? What action is needed: leverage, improve, or remove? Identify at least one underutilized resource you can better leverage this month, and one bottleneck you can address by improving organization or systems. Share your completed checklist with a team member, mentor, or advisor and discuss how you can get more strategic with what you already have.

Why this works: Organization starts with clarity about what's in your hands. By inventorying and strategically organizing your resources, you reduce stress, boost efficiency, and unlock new momentum for growth—all without needing to chase something new.

CHAPTER 9

BLUEPRINT FOR GROWTH
Your Strategic Navigation

The next morning, Ricki and Anthony followed the quiet murmur of conversation and cooking into the brightly lit kitchen. There were already stacks of blueberry pancakes in the middle of the table, surrounded by pitchers of water and orange juice, bowls of yogurt, and fresh berries. The smell of coffee hit Ricki right away, and she graciously accepted the steaming hot cup handed to her by Coach.

Once she had a little caffeine flowing through her veins, Ricki noticed that Coach wasn't in his usual attire. He had swapped out tennis shoes for hiking boots, his khaki shorts for long pants, and was wearing a light jacket over his signature polo.

"Going somewhere?" Ricki asked, gesturing to his outfit.

"Once a week I like to get up, have breakfast, and then head out for a hike. It helps keep me active, and I like to think of it as my time to think and reflect and connect with nature."

"That sounds nice," Anthony said, pouring homemade syrup on his pancakes.

"It is. It's a commitment I made to myself a while ago, and I like to stick with it."

"He goes rain or shine," Edna added.

"Would anyone like to go with me?" Coach asked, looking around the table.

"Can't today," said Clara from across the table. "We've got another meeting with that investor, and then Nate connected with somebody on social media who did the whole mobile coffee truck thing for a while and is looking to sell his truck. It feels like today could be the first day toward making this dream a reality!" She took another pancake from the stack and put it on her plate.

"And what about you two? Care to join me on a nature hike?" Coach asked, nodding to David and Darla.

"Oh, thanks for the invite, but we're heading back to New Jersey today. I called my dad and told him we were ready to listen," David said.

"We are so happy to hear that," Coach said before turning his attention to Ricki and Anthony, raising an eyebrow expectantly.

Ricki and Anthony looked at each other. They didn't have any set plans for the day, but Ricki had been looking forward to a day attacking their business strategy, working side by side with Anthony on their one-page plan, figuring out how to look at their one-year goals and break it down by quarter, by month, and maybe even by week so they'd have a clear, actionable path forward.

"I don't know. My brain is buzzing with information from the last few days, and I was looking forward to sitting down and trying to sort through it all. Figure out where to go next," Ricki said hesitantly.

Anthony looked over at Ricki. "I don't know, babe—I feel like we've learned so much from Coach already. Doesn't make sense to sit here and try to figure out the next steps on our own if there's an opportunity to learn from someone who's already done it . . ." He trailed off, his eyes hopeful. She knew he was right. The last few days with Coach had been so valuable, and turning down time to hear what he had to say and learn a few more lessons didn't make sense.

"Okay, yeah, a hike sounds good," Ricki said, sipping her coffee.

Coach smiled triumphantly. "Excellent. Go change into some comfortable shoes and clothes and meet me out on the porch in twenty minutes." Coach stood up, brought his plate to the sink, kissed his wife on the cheek, and retreated toward the back of the house.

Nineteen minutes later, Anthony and Ricki were seated in the rocking chairs, waiting for Coach. When he came through the screen door, the two stood up and started to make their way down the stairs and toward the driveway.

"Hold on—before we go, I want to give you a little information about this hike and make sure we have everything we need,"

Coach said, holding a hand up to stop them. Ricki and Anthony sat back down.

Coach explained that there were a lot of great trails nearby, offering a mix of coastal views, woodlands, and scenic landmarks. "We need to decide which trail we want to hike. I like to pick based on my current energy level, factor in how much time we have, and consider what my goals are for that particular hike. So, for me, I'm feeling like I've got a ton of energy, we've got all the time in the world, and I want to show you some incredible sights."

"I'm not an avid hiker per se," Anthony said, gesturing to his tall, bulky physique. "But I'm up for a challenge."

"And I love long hikes, but I don't think I want to do an all-day trek," Ricki added.

"In my experience, a shorter, less strenuous trail might be best if you're not sure of your endurance, while a longer, more challenging hike might be chosen if you want to push yourself. It's about weighing the pros and cons," said Coach.

"I say let's go for a shorter and less strenuous time, so we can talk, enjoy the views, and take our time," Anthony said confidently.

"I agree," Ricki said.

Coach nodded. "Next, we need to make sure we pack accordingly. Since we don't plan on being out all day, we don't need to overpack, but we will need water, snacks, and to put on a few layers."

Ricki took a second to observe the weather around her and thought her leggings and tank top would be perfect hiking attire. "Layers?" she asked.

"The weather changes quickly up here, and as the elevation changes, so do the temps. If you brought a jacket or long-sleeved shirt, I'd suggest running up to get it," Coach suggested. When they came back down with their jackets, Ricki noticed Coach had three lightweight backpacks lined up on the porch.

"We'll bring one water bottle for every hour of hiking, but we'll skip the heavy lunch items to keep our backpacks light." Coach dropped water bottles into each backpack. He pushed the backpacks toward Ricki and Anthony, who diligently slung them over their shoulders.

"When I take people on hikes, I also like to discuss energy management, so we're all on the same page about pacing ourselves," said Coach. "We agreed that this would be an easier hike, but we should all communicate our expectations for our pace. It would be a mess if some of us wanted to stop and look at every flower and rock when others wanted to beeline it and use it as a cardiovascular workout. When we get on the trail, we can experiment with different paces and walking speeds to make sure we avoid burning out too soon. We can agree on a system for brakes so that we can rest but still keep our momentum." Then, he added, "Before you build the strategy, you've got to build agreement. When you're not aligned, you'll waste time fighting each other instead of fighting for your business. Agreement—it's your accelerant. Without it, even the best strategies fall flat."

"How about a ten-minute break every hour to drink water and have a snack?" Anthony asked.

Coach smiled. "That's a great plan. And if we start our hike and realize that we need to take fewer breaks or make them longer, we can adjust.

"Recalibrate," Ricki chimed in, giving Anthony a wink.

When they arrived at the trailhead, Coach stood in front of a framed picture of the trail map. "This is one of my favorite trails because every time you hike it, it's different. The terrain can be unpredictable, and there are a lot of different ways to get to the same endpoint. I'm going to let you two take the lead here," Coach said, smiling as he watched panic and surprise come over their faces.

"Us? We're not hikers! We were just following you!" Anthony said nervously.

"I'll be here if you need me, but I'm confident that with the right tools"—he handed them a laminated map—"you'll figure it out. Let's go!" he said, sweeping his hand in a grand gesture to indicate they should go ahead.

Ricki looked at the map for a while, quietly discussed a few options with Anthony, and slid the map into her backpack. "Let's go!" she repeated, taking the first steps onto the trail.

The first twenty minutes of the walk were pretty quiet, as everyone got their bearings and took in the stunning trees. Ricki was so busy looking up that the sudden squishy feeling underneath her boots startled her. She stopped and noticed that the dirt trail had suddenly turned into a muddy one.

Ricki hesitated for a moment, considering their options. She glanced at Anthony, who was already testing the ground with his foot, looking for a way around the mud. They both realized quickly that the map wouldn't help them navigate this obstacle. "We can either try to avoid it, or we can push through," Ricki said, her voice calm despite the sudden challenge.

Anthony eyed the trail ahead, then the mud, his face scrunching in thought. "We might be able to find a path along the edge.

But if we just go straight through, we'll make it faster." He shifted his weight, preparing to make a decision.

"But we're not in a rush," Ricki countered, shifting her weight in her shoes. "So we could try and walk along the edge, hold onto the trees there, and avoid it," Ricki suggested, looking at Coach for support. He didn't offer any.

"Yeah. We could. Let's try," Anthony said. Ricki took a deep breath, remembering Coach's words about being adaptable. She looked for the driest sections of the path and planted her feet firmly, one in front of the other, while using the young tree branches for balance. She heard Coach and Anthony grunting and squishing behind her when the skinny branch she was holding snapped. She felt Anthony's hands instinctively shoot out to catch her, but she fell fast. She sat for a moment in the mud and took a deep breath. She felt anger start to bubble up, which she knew was really just coming from being embarrassed, and then took another deep breath. Anthony held out his hands to help her up.

"New plan. We just trudge through. It'll be easier than balancing on the slope. And that's what hiking boots are for, right?" she said to nobody in particular. She allowed Anthony to help her up, and then they were off, sloshing through the muddy trail one step at a time. Finally, the mud dried and they were back on the dirt trail.

"Now, I know you may not want to hear this," Coach's voice came from the back, "but I'm glad you fell."

Ricki stopped in her tracks. What did he just say?

"Hear me out," he said. "Back there you had to decide on going through the mud or trying to avoid it. You discussed which would be easier, made good points about effort and time, and made a decision. And guess what?"

"It was the wrong one," Ricki said, irritated, looking back at Coach.

"It was the wrong one," he confirmed. "But when plan A didn't work, you didn't just camp in the mud. You stood up, recalibrated, talked it through, and came up with a new plan that did work. And another thing. As you tried to balance on the edge, to skirt around the problem, it made me think of football."

"Of course it did," Ricki muttered under her breath

"In football, when you step out of bounds, when you move in a way that is outside the framework, what happens?"

"You get a penalty!" Anthony said proudly, missing the glare it earned him from Ricki.

"Right. There are penalties, and consequences, for navigating outside of the framework. Here the penalty was falling in the mud, but in business stepping out of bounds or ignoring the framework that is in place can have much more serious consequences. Okay, that's it. I'm done," Coach said, holding his hands up in mock surrender.

Ricki wanted to be mad, but she knew she had just learned a valuable lesson. Landing in the mud was embarrassing, inconvenient, and ineffective. It reminded her of some of the ways she tried to solve problems at the office. She'd see a problem, and then act on the first solution that she thought of, instead of taking the time to weigh the pros and cons, talk it over with Anthony, and decide on the most effective course of action. She also realized that they'd never be able to tell when they were going out of bounds if they didn't create the framework first.

They continued their hike, pointing out birds and wildlife and listening to Coach as he taught them about the history of the area. When they got to a fork in the road, Anthony pulled the laminated map out of Ricki's bag and looked it over.

"The Sunflower Trail will take us in a loop around this big body of water, and bring us back to the parking lot. The Rosebud Trail will take us all the way over here, a bit out of the way, but it says there is a scenic lookout," Anthony said, running his finger over the map.

Ricki looked at her watch. "We were making pretty good time until the mud incident, so I think before we pick a trail we need to take stock and determine how we're doing so far, how we are feeling, and what we need to do to get back to the car before we're all exhausted."

"The Rosebud Trail looks like it's a little bit steeper," Anthony said, pointing to the elevation change marker on the map. "So we should factor that in when it comes to how long it will take us. If we want to do the scenic route and see the lookout, we should either pick up our pace so that we get there sooner, or stick to the Sunflower Trail and save the lookout for another day."

Anthony could see that Coach was listening intently to their conversation. He realized that this was exactly why he wanted to bring them on this hike and that all this problem-solving was not just a natural part of going on a hike, but an intentional lesson in strategy. In true Coach style, he just stood there and waited. It was up to Ricki and Anthony to make the final decision.

"I'm muddy, and I think I'm ready to be at the end of this hike. I vote for doing the Sunflower Trail," Ricki said confidently.

Anthony nodded in agreement, as did Coach, and they turned right to follow the trail marker marked with a bright yellow sunflower.

The trio talked, laughed, and told stories as they followed the dirt trail around a gorgeous lake dotted with lily pads and surrounded by towering trees. When they got to an exceptionally beautiful part of the lake, Anthony took out his phone and started taking pictures. Ricki found herself getting a little bit irritated, wondering why he was stopping now when they were so close to the car.

"Okay, Mr. National Geographic, you got your pictures. Let's keep moving. We said we'd spend three hours on this hike, and we are . . ." Ricki looked at her watch. "Right at the two-point-five-hour mark." She started to walk ahead and noticed they weren't following.

"Hello? Did you hear me? Car is this way," she said, pointing to the parking lot in the distance.

"Yes, babe, I heard you. But come here. Look at the water! And with those trees over there and the sky, it's just incredible. Come take a picture with me," Anthony said, looking excited.

Ricki sighed and half-stomped over to her waiting husband. "I feel like we've spent so much of this hike weighing options and prioritizing steps," she said, trying not to sound like a brat.

"But that's part of having a strategy," Coach said gently. "It's not always about having a fixed plan but about adjusting according to the moment. And this is a beautiful moment," he added, nodding toward Anthony, who was standing in front of the lake, waiting for Ricki to slide in next to him for a picture.

Ricki took a deep breath and found her spot tucked beside her husband. She smiled as Coach took the picture, and when she went to pull away from Anthony, he held her closer. Together they stood in silence, taking in the scenery. He kissed the top of her head, and Ricki felt a shift. She was still focused on the plan, but the plan didn't have to be rigid. The key was in the ability to change direction when necessary, and in knowing when to pause and take in the view, even when you had your eyes set on something else.

"Thanks for the reminder," she said to Anthony with a smile, her voice softer now. "I think I needed that."

When they arrived back at the bed and breakfast, the house was quiet. Edna met them on the porch and asked them about their adventure. "I'll tell you all about it later," said Ricki, breezing past Edna and into the house. "I've got to get these muddy clothes off and take a shower!" she laughed.

Coach took the three backpacks and disappeared around the house, leaving Edna and Anthony sitting in silence on the porch.

"So, how'd it go?" she asked after a few moments.

"Well, you probably already knew this, but it was an elaborate plan to get Ricki and me to understand the value of having a strategy," Anthony said, shooting Edna a knowing glance. She nodded and smiled, waiting for him to continue.

"He basically left us to our own devices out there. But when it's just me and Ricki and we need to figure things out, we can do it. We listened to each other, and we weighed the pros and cons of each decision that we made. When she fell in the mud, I didn't say, 'I told you so,' like I would have in the past. Instead, I just helped her up, and we made a new plan to move forward together. She struggled a bit with staying committed to a deadline, but man oh man, that Sunflower Trail . . ."

"Oh, by the water? Breathtaking, isn't it? I could sit there all day," Edna replied.

"I couldn't just walk by it. I had to stay and take it all in," Anthony said, agreeing. "And I know it's hard for Ricki sometimes to stop and enjoy the view, but that hike helped us to remember the importance of it. We had a plan and a strategy, but we had to figure out what part of it was rigid and what could be flexible. Eventually, I got her to come stand with me and just take it all in. I think Coach got a few good pictures. It's something that I'll remember forever," Anthony said with a smile. "I think it did something for us. Reminded us that we're a good team and that it's not about having the perfect plan—it's just about having a plan and being willing to adjust it in real time."

They sat in silence for a bit, and then Anthony added, "And I was just thinking, we were able to be successful on that hike because we had a few things. We had Coach, a map, and a plan before we got there. If I think about our business, right now it feels like we're going into it without any of those things. We don't have a set direction, a map, a compass—anything that's pointing us toward our destination."

Edna looked at him, an impressed look coming over her. "That's a great analogy, Anthony. It sounds like you're noticing that you guys have been reacting more than you have been planning.

Acknowledging it and noticing it is the first step. Now that you know that's where you're struggling, you can fix it and move forward."

"Are David and Darla still here?" Anthony asked, noticing the Mercedes was not in the driveway.

"No, they left a little while ago. I'm not sure what Coach said to them, but they seemed to have a newfound confidence about taking over the business. Darla even mentioned maybe taking a job there too, so they could both learn the ins and outs of the business and tackle it together. Coach sure can work that magic," Edna said with a slight shake of her head.

A little while later, Ricki appeared on the couch, freshly showered and without a speck of mud on her. Nate and Clara joined them a little later. Coach was the last one to join them, and as the sun set, Ricki couldn't help but feel emotional. Here she was, in this beautiful place, surrounded by strangers who had already taught her so much about herself and her business. She sat and listened as everyone talked excitedly about their achievements of the day, and Anthony's retelling of Ricki's muddy mishap had everyone in stitches.

After a while, a wave of exhaustion settled over Anthony, and he stood up from the porch swing. "I'm going to call it a day, everybody. I'm glad everyone had such a productive day. It's one I'll remember forever, that's for sure."

"I'll come with you," Ricki said, reaching for Anthony's hand. Everyone said their good nights, and the couple headed back to the Tulip Room for some well-deserved sleep.

The essence of strategy is choosing what not to do.

—Michael Porter[3]

ACTION STEP

To put strategic thinking into action, download and complete the Revenue Strategy Map Worksheet by scanning the following QR code or visiting accelerateplaybook.com. This tool is designed to help you clarify and align your key growth activities across three critical areas: OFFER, ATTRACT, and CONVERT.

OFFER: Define exactly what you're selling (product/service), your pricing, and your target sales quantities.

ATTRACT: Identify the marketing channels you'll use, set specific weekly actions (like social media posts or outreach), and determine how often you'll promote your offer.

CONVERT: Track your conversion rates, assign resources (such as team members or tools), and note any follow-up actions or special considerations.

How to use this tool: Set aside focused time this week to fill out each section of the worksheet with your current or planned strategies. Use the worksheet to get clear on your revenue goals, marketing efforts, and sales process—ensuring every part of your growth plan is intentional and measurable. Post your completed Revenue Strategy Map somewhere visible, and review it weekly to track progress, adjust your actions, and stay accountable. Share your map with a mentor, advisor, or your team to gather feedback and refine your strategy as you go.

Why this matters: Utilizing the Revenue Strategy Map transforms abstract goals into a concrete, actionable plan. It brings clarity to your growth strategy, aligns your team, and helps you focus on the activities that directly drive revenue—making your business more strategic, resilient, and successful.

CHAPTER 10

THE MAIN THING
Mastering What Matters Most

The next morning, after another delicious breakfast, Ricki and Anthony were sipping coffee on the porch when they heard a car come crunching up the gravel driveway. *Wow,* Ricki thought as a tall man in a baseball cap approached them, *Who is this?* She took in the man's built physique and salt-and-pepper beard. He made his way up onto the porch with a warm smile and introduced himself as Todd.

"I'm here to see Coach, to give him some of these," he said, holding up a few glossy brochures. On the front, a family was enjoying a sunny boat day, surrounded by crystal clear blue waters and a smiling boat captain at the helm. Just then, the screen door screeched, and Edna came bursting out, her arms outstretched to welcome Todd.

"Todd! So good to see you. This is Ricki and Anthony—they're staying with us for a while."

"I told Coach I'd swing by with these today," Todd said to Edna. "I appreciate you letting me leave them here. I've definitely seen an uptick in business since I dropped off the last batch," Todd added with a smile, handing the brochures to Edna.

"Oh, it's our pleasure. We love recommending you to guests. They always come back sun-kissed and happy. Do you want to come in? Coach should be here soon," Edna said, gesturing toward the front door.

Just then, Coach's booming voice came from inside and he materialized at the screen door. "Captain Todd!" Coach said with a big smile, stepping onto the porch and shaking Todd's hand.

"Coach. So good to see you. How are things?"

"Can't complain," Coach replied. "Weather is great, got great guests staying with us this week—" He gestured to Ricki and Anthony. "Life is good!"

"Glad to hear it. Hey, we just had a cancellation for a ride this afternoon. Any chance you and your friends would want to come out on the water today?" Todd asked, looking at both couples. "I could show you the most beautiful sights in the Vineyard," Todd added, lifting his brows.

"A boat day sounds great! Ricki, Anthony? What do you say? It's a great way to see the area. And Captain Todd is the best captain in the area. I've known him for years, and his tours are always a lot of fun."

Anthony looked at Ricki, who was already nodding. "Let's do it!" Ricki said, and Todd lifted his hand to high-five her.

"What about Nate and Clara? Should we see if they want to join too?" Coach asked, looking around for their van.

"They're already out for the day. I connected them with Deja—she's going to help them create a business plan," Edna said proudly.

"That's great! Deja is a great resource, and she'll be able to help them immensely. She's so good at that stuff, and her several successful businesses here on Martha's Vineyard are proof!" Coach said, looking at Ricki and Anthony.

"Meet me at the marina in an hour?" Todd asked, already making his way off the porch and back to his car.

Thirty minutes later, Ricki and Anthony met Coach and Edna on the porch. Edna had swapped her cat apron for a big floppy hat, and a modest black swimsuit under a floral coverup. Instead of his official coaching getup, Coach looked ready for a beach day in bright teal swim trunks, a faded Martha's Vineyard tank top, and flip flops. They looked like quite the couple.

They drove together to Edgartown Harbor, and when they arrived, Edna, Ricki, and Anthony stood on the dock looking out over the water, the incredible luxury yachts bobbing in the water. Coach walked into the small office building and came back out with Captain Todd, who led them to *Matilda*, a "classic fifty-three-foot Hatteras motor yacht," Todd explained proudly as he stood with one foot on the boat and one on the dock and held out his hand to help the ladies on board.

Ricki and Anthony were no strangers to luxury yachts, as they'd attended many parties on the water during Anthony's NFL days, but it had been a while, and Anthony couldn't help but smile as he boarded. "A tour?" Todd asked, moving from the aft deck to the salon, gesturing for them to follow.

They stepped into the main salon, where rich teak paneling and plush seating created an inviting atmosphere. The large windows flooded the space with natural light, offering panoramic views of the marina. Todd continued, leading them down a few steps into the galley and dinette area.

"Three staterooms," Todd said, opening a door to reveal a cozy guest cabin. "The master's aft," Todd said, gesturing toward the beautiful master suite. Anthony looked down at Ricki and lifted his eyebrows suggestively. She playfully smacked his arm and followed Todd forward. Todd introduced them to Viv, a gorgeous Black woman in her thirties, standing confidently and flawless in a crisp, white uniform with navy accents. "Welcome aboard!" she said. "Once we get out on the water, I'll bring out some drinks and hors d'oeuvres."

The tour concluded on the flybridge, where Todd pointed out the helm station and the cushioned seating area—"Perfect for taking in the view," he said, and Anthony could tell he really loved his job. "She's got timeless charm, and she's built for comfort and adventure," Todd said, and Ricki wondered how many times he'd given this spiel to guests.

"So, what do you think? Should we take her out?" Todd finally asked. Everyone nodded enthusiastically and found their seats while Captain Todd found his place at the helm. Quiet "yacht rock" started streaming out of the speakers, and Ricki scooted closer to Anthony.

"Now, this is going to be a great day, but safety must always be the top priority," Captain Todd said, his voice turning serious. "Even though Viv and I have done this a hundred times, we have a comprehensive safety checklist. We check safety gear, review navigation routes, and make sure everyone knows the safety protocols before setting sail." Just then, Coach and Edna appeared from inside the cabin and sat across from Ricki and Anthony.

"You might be here to relax, enjoy the views, and have a good time, but if we don't get the basics right, none of that is possible," Captain Todd went on. "Safety isn't just something we do at the start, it's something we carry with us all day." Anthony couldn't help but notice the stark difference between this serious captain and the high-fiving, casual dude in a baseball cap they'd met just a few hours earlier. Todd turned his attention to the boat's dashboard, checking fluid levels and other systems.

"It's the same in life, really. You've got to prioritize what matters most. You can't get caught up in everything else and forget the fundamentals, or things can go off course before you even realize it," Coach said, giving Ricki and Anthony a knowing smile. Anthony watched as Viv and Captain Todd moved seamlessly across the vessel, like a well-oiled machine. It was like a synchronized dance, the way they confirmed the right number of life jackets, checked the pumps and navigation lights, and carefully addressed their inventory. Ricki watched Coach as he watched the team, and could tell his wheels were spinning. Keeping her eyes on Coach, she counted down in her head. *5, 4, 3, 2 . . .*

"You know," Coach started, and Ricki smiled to herself. She *knew* Coach was going to find a way to turn this into a learning opportunity.

Everyone turned their attention to Coach. "This here is the perfect example of how prioritization works—whether you're on a yacht, in business, or on the football field," he said, winking at Anthony. "On a boat, there is so much that goes into planning and making sure the basics are covered. Most of the time, we get on someone's boat and don't even think about all of the work and time that was put into making sure the trip was not just fun, but safe. Like out on the football field, we can't just call plays without making sure we have a solid defense, a clear strategy, and a game plan. We could have the best players in the league on our team, but if we don't prioritize the basics, it all falls apart. In business, same thing," he said, gesturing with his hands.

"We can't 'set sail'"—he used air quotes for this—"or grow, or scale, or accelerate, if we're not taking care of the fundamentals. It won't work if we don't look at each aspect of our business." He gestured to Viv and Todd as they methodically checked each system on the boat. "And we have to make sure we're prepared for what's ahead. For you guys, it's taking a good look at team morale, customer satisfaction, operational systems, and making sure those are solid before you think about expanding. And not just one look. You have to constantly have your eyes on these things. Because if they start to fail, you want to know sooner rather than later, right?"

Anthony nodded just as Captain Todd announced, "Okay! We're good to go!" They all watched as the experienced captain expertly maneuvered the huge vessel out of the marina and out into open water.

They sat mostly in silence for a while, taking in the stunning scenery and pointing out the gorgeous waterfront mansions and the lighthouse in the distance. A few minutes later, Viv appeared with a tray of bubbling champagne flutes. They all took a glass and toasted. As she sipped, Ricki looked over at Anthony and could tell by his expression that he was deep in thought.

"What are you thinking about?" she asked, moving closer to him.

"I was thinking about what Coach said about priorities. And if I had to make a checklist, what would the top three things be that I think we should be consistently evaluating? And I thought it would be our customers, our products, and our service. Do you agree?"

Ricki thought it over for a second and nodded.

"So if we keep pushing them to the bottom of the list, it's like ignoring the safety protocols on this boat. Everything else will eventually come crashing down." He looked at her with a serious look in his eyes. "I think sometimes we—well, definitely me—I just assume that as long as it's working, that it's working. But that's more reactive than proactive. I think we can start being more proactive in making the main thing the main thing."

"Oh, I like that," Ricki said, squeezing his arm. "Keeping the main thing the main thing. And for us that means maintaining customer relationships and making sure all of our systems are working."

Anthony was going to respond when the sound of Coach and Captain Todd's laughter erupted from the helm. When he could finally speak, Captain Todd said, "Coach and I were just reminiscing about the first time we were out on the boat together."

"I couldn't *stand* this man," Coach said, using his finger to jab Captain Todd in the chest. "We came out here for a private party—a friend of ours was having a birthday and hired this dude to charter a yacht for a night on the water. And from the moment we boarded, I knew this guy was going to be a piece of work."

"The whole time," Edna piped in, "he was loud and obnoxious. He played his own playlist and didn't let us have a say in what we listened to! The birthday girl had a whole itinerary with where she wanted to go and things she wanted to see . . ." Edna trailed off, looking accusingly at Todd. He looked down sheepishly and gestured for her to continue. "This guy had a plan of his own. He was Mr. Big Shot. Mr. Look-At-Me-I've-Got-A-Boat. Am I right?" she asked, looking at Todd again.

He nodded. "I was a different guy back then. I was so focused on me and my experience, so caught up in finally reaching my dream of owning a boat like this, that I made every experience about what I wanted to do. It fed my ego to have this nice boat and people to pay me to get on it. I thought I knew so much more than them about boats and the area in general, and I let them know. It's taken a lot of time, and therapy, to work through all that mess. I'm different now, though!" he said, throwing his hands up as if to indicate surrender.

"Man, I can't picture you like that," Anthony said.

"I know," Captain Todd replied. "It's embarrassing to think about. But these two sure know how to leave a scathing review," he said, pointing to Edna and Coach, "and I got a few other bad ones for the trips after that. I realized I wasn't going to stay in business very long if I kept it up. So I did some soul searching and spent some time with this one"—he put his arm around Coach's shoulder—"and got my stuff together. I learned that I have to know my customer. It has to be all about them and what they want. I even want to know when they're unhappy, because it lets me know what needs to change. Knowing my customer has been my top priority ever since."

"There's that word again," Anthony noticed. "Priority."

"Sometimes we think that everything is a priority, and when we try to get to it all, some of it inevitably falls through the cracks," Coach added. "Prioritizing is a fundamental part of recalibrating because it forces you to focus on what truly matters. It helps you cut through the noise, eliminate distractions, and align your actions with your goals. When you prioritize, you're not just reacting to everything that comes your way, you're taking intentional steps toward what will have the greatest impact. In business, in life, or even on this boat, prioritizing ensures that your time, energy, and resources are spent on the things that will move the needle. Without it, you risk spreading yourself too thin, chasing too many things at once, and losing sight of what's most important. Prioritization is what keeps you grounded, on track, and moving forward with clarity and purpose."

Everyone on the boat nodded in silent agreement. Captain Todd turned up the music (after making sure everyone agreed with his playlist) and maneuvered the boat into the outer harbor. Viv appeared again and invited everyone inside for hors d'oeuvres.

As they sat together and enjoyed a light snack and a stunning view, Ricki turned to Edna and asked, "How do you really figure out what should be a priority and what shouldn't? Sometimes everything feels urgent and important, and it's hard to know where to focus. And what if I think something is a priority but Anthony doesn't?"

Edna smiled and pulled a pen out of her purse. She motioned for Coach to pass her a napkin, and he slid one across the table to her. "Have you heard of the decision-making matrix?" she asked, drawing one line vertically down the napkin and another one across it, creating four separate sections.

"In college, maybe, but remind me," Ricki said.

"Here's the idea: You focus your energy on what's both urgent and important. You plan for the things that are important but not urgent. You delegate the urgent but not important tasks, and you let go of anything that's neither."

Ricki stayed quiet, watching Edna's hand quickly label each quadrant on the napkin.

"So part of recalibrating is taking the time to decide which tasks go in each quadrant. The goal is to have a plan in place for the things that are important but not urgent—"

"Babe, come here," Ricki interrupted, waving Anthony over to her. "Listen to this. If we want to be better about prioritizing, we need to use this matrix to decide where our focus needs to go."

Edna continued. "So what tasks would you say are important but not urgent?"

"Building relationships with existing customers. Training employees often," Anthony said, counting on his fingers.

"And what about improving strategic partnerships?" Ricki asked. Anthony nodded in agreement.

"Okay, great," Edna said, writing them down in the quadrant marked "important but not urgent." "So you put plans and systems in place to make sure they are done and done well. What about things that are urgent but not important?" Edna asked, pointing to the next quadrant.

"Maybe filing, printing reports, posting on social media? These things have to get done quickly, but they don't necessarily contribute to moving the needle," Anthony said.

"Okay, well, I think we're guilty of scheduling too many meetings that could be emails," Ricki pointed out. "We need to communicate with our team, but it doesn't always have to be a meeting."

"What about work around the shop? Like fixing light bulbs. We have to do it so the guys can see what they're doing, but it's not vital for the overall workflow," Anthony added.

Edna wrote the answers down and said, "So you delegate those. You find someone who can handle these tasks consistently. They need to get done, but they don't need *your* full attention, because your attention is up here." Edna tapped the pen on the "urgent and important" section. "Can I make a suggestion? What about having conversations with non-decision-makers, without a goal or expectation in mind of how it benefits the business? Would you consider that?"

"Oh, that's a good one," said Ricki. "Yes. I like that. Sometimes we're so focused on making sure everyone feels heard that there's too many voices and too many opinions. That makes it hard to gain clarity and find a solution."

"We should define who the decision-makers are, then, right?" Anthony asked.

"Yeah. I mean, you and I have the final say, but the managers make decisions in their departments, and so their input is valuable too," Ricki said, and she found herself smiling.

"What?" Anthony asked, noticing her changed expression.

"I just really feel like a team with you right now. I love this. I love figuring stuff out with you." She smiled, laying her head on his shoulder.

They continued working the matrix, brainstorming tasks and responsibilities that had to happen in order for their business to run smoothly, and discussed which task went where. When they were done, the napkin looked a little chaotic, but Ricki looked at it and felt peace. There, on that napkin, was the map she needed. It was a physical representation of what she needed to focus on and what she needed to let go.

"Can I take this?" Ricki asked, reaching for the napkin. Edna slid it over to her, and Ricki pulled out her playbook from her purse and copied the napkin into the playbook. Anthony looked up at Edna, who winked at him and then excused herself from the table and went back out onto the boat deck.

The rest of the afternoon was spent lazily coasting through the harbor, soaking up the sun, and enjoying bottomless drinks and gourmet appetizers. The music was good, the scenery was breathtaking, and the conversation flowed from travel and business to football and food. Captain Todd was an excellent captain, making sure everyone was having fun but also paying close attention to his surroundings, the systems of the boat, the weather, and all of the logistics to ensure a relaxing and safe day on the water.

When it was time to head back, Ricki needed a little help getting off the boat. She hadn't had that much champagne in a while, and her head was feeling a little buzzy. Anthony gently guided her off the boat and down the dock, where they said their goodbyes to Captain Todd. Anthony opened the car door for Ricki with a big smile on his face.

"Now, what are you smiling about?" Ricki asked, pulling on her seatbelt. Anthony closed the door and came around to the driver's seat.

"I just haven't seen you buzzed in a while. I forgot how cute you are when you're tipsy. And," he said, putting the car in reverse, "I love being on a team with you, too. I loved working through that matrix with you, putting on paper what we need to do. Makes me excited to get home and put all of it into action."

He followed Coach and Edna as they pulled out of the marina and headed back to the bed and breakfast. Ricki rested her head on the window and smiled to herself. Even though her mind was a little fuzzy thanks to the champagne, she couldn't remember the last time she'd felt this clear about what needed to be done. *We've been so caught up in putting out fires that we've been missing the bigger picture*, she thought. *If we can focus on what truly matters—our customers, our products, and the experience we're creating—everything else will fall into place.*

She glanced over at Anthony, who was humming along to the music, his excitement contagious. *We've got a good team*, she thought. *And now we've got a clear game plan. Time to make it happen.*

The key is not to prioritize what's on your schedule, but to schedule your priorities.

—Stephen Covey, *The 7 Habits of Highly Effective People*

ACTION STEP

Complete the Brain Dump Worksheet by scanning the following QR code or visiting accelerateplaybook.com.

Dump It All: Begin by listing every task, responsibility, and idea currently on your mind—big or small—using the Brain Dump Worksheet provided in this chapter.

Sort Using the Matrix: Categorize each item using the Decision-Making Matrix (Urgent vs. Important) to visually clarify what truly matters.

Let Go of the Rest: Identify tasks that are distractions or low priority. Delegate, automate, or eliminate these to free up your time and energy.

Focus & Revisit: Highlight your top priorities and commit to focusing on these first. Schedule a weekly review of your Brain Dump and Matrix to make prioritization a continuous habit.

Why this works: Prioritization is not a one-time event—it's a discipline that brings clarity, reduces overwhelm, and ensures your daily actions align with your biggest goals. By making this process rou-  tine, you'll create space for real progress and sustainable business growth.

CHAPTER 11

THE AUTOMATION ADVANTAGE
Building Your Scalable Playbook

A buzzing sound brought Anthony out of a deep sleep. It quieted and then started again. Frustrated, he sat up in bed, wiped his eyes, and tried to clear the sleep from his mind. There it was again, the buzzing. He looked across the room to the desk and saw his phone dancing across the surface. He stood up and looked at his phone: six missed calls, all from the office. *This can't be good*, he thought, pressing the key to listen to the voicemail and putting the phone to his ear.

Message one: Hey Anthony, it's Crystal. I hope you're having fun on your trip. I hate to bother you while you're away, but I just got into the office, and there are a few messages here from George Brown, saying something about a delivery that never showed up for his work trucks. I don't see anything about it in the system and wanted to check in with you before I called him. Get back to me when you can.

Message two: Hey Anthony, sorry—me again. Just checking to see if you know anything about Mr. Brown's order? I hope it's okay, but I checked your calendar on your desk and saw his name down and an order number but nothing else. Call me back when you can.

Message three: Anthony, it's Crystal. I don't know what you want me to do. Mr. Brown called and he's really upset and—

Anthony ended the voicemail and looked over at Ricki, fast asleep. He hated to wake her, especially with bad news. He paced the bedroom for a minute, tapping the phone against his palm. He took a deep breath, stepped out onto the patio, and called Crystal back. She answered on the first ring, sounding flustered. He could hear a few male voices in the background, and while he couldn't make out what they were saying, he could tell that the conversation was tense.

"So sorry I missed all your calls, Crystal," Anthony said quickly. "What's going on?"

In a shaky voice, Crystal explained that George Brown, a long-term customer, had emailed a few times last night and that morning, wondering about a tire order that he'd made a few weeks ago for his fleet of work trucks. He had an order number written down on a piece of paper, but it didn't match anything that they had in the system. After not receiving any response, he'd called a few times and become more and more belligerent, and then minutes ago had showed up at the office.

Anthony listened in horror. Was Crystal in danger? What was this guy doing, showing up at his place of business and intimidating his staff?

"Do you feel like you're in danger?" Anthony asked, his heart rate starting to accelerate. "Are Antwon and Chris there?"

"Yeah, they are here. They're talking to him and he's calming down. But he keeps saying that it was a big order and a lot of money and that you said you were going to revise an order and get back to him . . ." Crystal trailed off.

Then it hit him. He knew exactly what Crystal was talking about. Anthony's stomach sank as the realization hit him like a freight train. The revised order. The conversation. The promise he'd made to George Brown to "get it handled." It all came rushing back. He had scribbled a note on his desk calendar but never logged it into the system. In the chaos of preparing for the trip and juggling other tasks, he had completely forgotten to follow through.

"Crystal, listen," Anthony said, his voice low but firm, "this is my fault. I dropped the ball. I remember talking to George about revising his order, but I didn't get it entered into the system. That's on me."

There was a brief pause on the other end of the line, and then Crystal exhaled. "Okay. So, what should I tell him? He's still asking for an update, and he doesn't look like he's leaving until he gets an answer."

Anthony put his hands on his head and paced the patio. "Alright, here's what we're going to do. First, tell George I'll personally call him in the next thirty minutes to sort this out. Apologize on my behalf and let him know we're working on a solution."

Crystal hesitated. "You're sure? He's pretty angry, Anthony."

"I'm sure," he said firmly. "Tell him I'll take full responsibility and make it right. And Crystal, thanks for handling this. I know it's a tough situation."

He hung up the phone and leaned against the patio railing. He took a deep breath and walked back inside. The sound of the sliding glass door woke Ricki up, and she looked at him, confused. "Everything okay?" she asked. When he didn't answer, she could tell by his face that something was wrong. "What? What happened?" she asked, sitting up in bed.

Anthony hated to be the bearer of bad news, especially since their trip had been going so well and he really felt like they were getting back on track. He sat on the edge of the bed and explained everything. Instinctively, he waited for her to get up and start shouting about how useless he was and how she had to take care of everything, or how this always happened. But instead, she took a deep breath and put her hand on his leg.

"Okay. We can handle this. You said you'd call him back in thirty minutes?" she asked. Anthony nodded. Ricki stood up and went to the dresser. "Let me get dressed and let's go downstairs. We'll get some quick advice from Coach on how to handle this, and we can call George together, okay, babe?" she asked, as she rifled through her drawers.

Anthony quickly descended the stairs and found Coach and Edna drinking coffee in the kitchen.

"Sorry Anthony, late start on breakfast this morning. I can whip up some cereal if you're hungry," Edna said, starting to stand.

"Oh, no, thank you," Anthony replied. "I actually wondered if we could get your help with something. We have a bit of a work emergency."

Coach pulled the chair out next to him and Anthony sat down. He quickly retold the story of the phone call and the hectic day that George Brown had called with his massive commercial order, how he wrote it down but didn't put it in the system, and that he was a big deal customer who they really couldn't afford to lose.

"And," Anthony added, "I have to call him back in"—he looked at his watch—"twenty-six minutes with a solution." Just then, Ricki came rushing into the kitchen and sat down next to Anthony.

"Okay, we don't have enough time to teach you the importance of having systems in twenty-six minutes. That's going to come after we call this guy back, take accountability for our actions, make sure he feels heard, and come to a solution that shows him we value his business," Coach said directly. Anthony pulled out his phone.

"Wait, wait, wait," Coach said, putting his hand on Anthony's arm. "Just because this is important and urgent doesn't mean we go into it without a plan. You're not going to be able to fix the mistake from here. But you are going to handle it in a way that shows you value his business. That's what builds trust, even when you mess up."

Anthony looked at his watch again. Twenty-four minutes.

"Over the years we've created a pretty good system for fixing problems," Edna said, folding her hands on the table. "First, we start with a genuine apology. This will be easy because I can already tell that you guys are really sorry that this slipped through the cracks. So we're not just going to say 'sorry'—we're going to say, 'I apologize for dropping the ball on this,' and show that you're committed to making it right."

"Okay," Anthony said. "I did tell Crystal to apologize to Mr. Brown for me, but I'll make sure to apologize to him directly when I call him back."

Coach nodded. "Then we're going to lay out a clear solution. Is there a way for you to process the revised order from here?" Coach asked.

"Yes. I can do it from my laptop," Ricki said.

"Great. So we'll tell him that the revised order is going to be processed right away and that you will expedite shipping? Is that something you can do?"

"Absolutely," Anthony replied.

"And then we're not just going to stop there. We're going to fix the problem but we're also going to continue the conversation and ask for feedback."

"Oh, I have a feeling I know what kind of feedback he's going to give us," Anthony said, looking worried.

"And that's okay," said Coach. "Feedback is feedback. We can't just listen to the people who love us and think we're doing great—it's important to listen to the people who think we can do better. It's not always fun to hear, but it's important so that we can get better at what we do."

"I think asking him for feedback right now is just going to make him more mad," Ricki countered.

"Not if you frame it the right way," Coach said. "Something like, 'We want to make sure this never happens again, so we'd love to hear if there's anything we can do to improve your experience moving forward.' It makes him part of the solution, and people like feeling heard."

Anthony and Ricki looked at each other. Coach had some good ideas, but he didn't know Mr. Brown. Mr. Brown was a loyal customer, yes, but he was also very particular, and when he was disappointed, he let you know, along with the rest of the world, via Google reviews.

"Trust us," Edna said, noticing their worried glances.

"And after the call, we're going to have a nice long conversation about the importance of having systems. Knowing how to systemize your business is one of the key fundamentals in moving forward," Coach said. "It's also an important step in the recalibration process. Just like right now, instead of jumping right back into the phone call unprepared, we took a few minutes to recalibrate and think about what we wanted to say and how we wanted to handle it. We will come off as more confident and competent this way."

Anthony looked at his watch again. Ten minutes.

Coach leaned back in his chair, studying Anthony. "How are you feeling about this? You ready to own it and turn this around?"

Anthony nodded, took a deep breath, stood up, and walked out to the porch. Ricki followed.

||||||||||||

"So . . . how'd it go?" Coach asked ten minutes later when Anthony and Ricki came back into the kitchen.

"Well, he's mad. And understandably so," Ricki said. "But he's willing to give us another chance. We told him that we would process the order now, and expedite delivery, and I'm about to go upstairs and do that now on my laptop."

"And did he offer any feedback?" Coach asked.

"Oh, he had feedback" Ricki half laughed. "Pay more attention, do a better job, get it right next time, don't be so disorganized . . ." she trailed off.

"Well, he's not wrong," Coach said gently, shrugging his shoulders. "But hey, he did say he'd allow you to fix it, right? That's good news. So as long as you don't drop the ball on this part, and you provide a solution, I have a feeling you won't lose his business. And, since you're about to learn all about the importance of creating systems, you'll run into these big problems a lot less often moving forward."

"Hallelujah for that," Anthony sighed. Ricki put her hands on the table and stood up. "I'm going to go process that order now," she said, disappearing upstairs. Anthony put his head in his hands.

"Hey," said Coach, "give yourself grace. You made a mistake. You're human. You were accountable for the role you played in it, and you found a solution. That's all you can do. Use this feeling to remind you that you don't want to feel like this again, and work to put systems in place that will prevent it." Coach slapped Anthony on the back.

A little while later, breakfast was served, the order was processed, and the kitchen was buzzing again with quiet conversation and the smell of Edna's famous blueberry pancakes. After they ate, Nate and Clara disappeared from the kitchen and came back a few minutes later with their suitcases.

"Well, we hate to eat and run, but we're about to hit the road," Nate announced, standing in the kitchen doorway.

"Let's all see them out," Edna said, wiping her hands on her apron. The whole group moved out to the porch, exchanging hugs with Nate and Clara and offering them well wishes on their coffee adventure.

"Thank you for the hospitality and the amazing pancakes. But thank you more for the wisdom and advice that you offered to us while we were here," Clara said, looking at Edna and Coach. "We will use everything we learned on this trip to make this business a success. Once we get the coffee truck up and running, all of you get free coffee for life!" Clara said with a big smile.

Edna and Coach walked them to their van while Ricki and Anthony watched from the porch. Coach and Edna whispered a few quiet words to the couple and then watched as the van disappeared down the gravel driveway.

"I hope they do it," Ricki said, watching the van drive away.

"Me too," Coach said thoughtfully, wrapping his hand around Edna's waist. "They've got potential for sure. They just need to remember the fundamentals."

"And keep that van organized!" Edna added, and everyone laughed.

Coach looked at Anthony and Ricki. "Let's systemize," he said, a big smile crossing his face.

"Let's systemize," Anthony repeated, and followed Coach back inside.

Instead of walking into the kitchen, Coach walked down the main hallway and gestured for Ricki and Anthony to follow. They followed him into a spacious office, complete with a beautiful oak desk, floor-to-ceiling bookshelves, and football memorabilia on almost every available surface. Right away Ricki looked at the framed photos hanging on the wall; they were of Coach in every stage of his life: playing football, coaching football, wedding photos, travel photos, family photos. Coach rolled a whiteboard from the corner of the room to the center and stood in front of it.

Immediately Anthony was transported back to his football days, crowded around a bunch of big, sweaty men listening intently to their coach, who wrote Xs and Os and squiggly lines all across the whiteboard to demonstrate different plays and strategies.

"As you know, the playbook is the foundation of everything we do in football," said Coach. "It's not just random plays, it's a well-thought-out guide that ensures everyone on the field knows their role and executes it seamlessly. Without it, players are confused, and chaos takes over. Your business needs a playbook too. You need a system that ensures every person and process operates like clockwork. If your coach showed up without a playbook, you'd have a lot of questions, right?" he asked. They both nodded.

"You two are athletes. This fundamental principle, systemization, has been ingrained in you since you were little. You know how to do it. You both excelled on the field because you had systems in place. So you just need to do it with your business. Today, we're going to make a playbook."

Anthony and Ricki looked at each other in excitement.

"Anthony, when you were out on that field, did your team just make up plays willy-nilly? Just get out there and randomly decide to do a pass play or T formation?" Coach asked.

"No, the plays were already decided," Anthony replied. "We had practiced with them—all we had to do was call them out, and everybody understood what they needed to do."

"Exactly. And that's what your business needs. Repeatable strategies that everybody knows and everybody understands. Not quick-fix answers made under pressure."

Coach turned to the whiteboard and started writing, and Edna appeared out of nowhere and handed them two pocket-size composition notebooks and pencils. They smiled up at her and Ricki mouthed, "Thank you."

Ricki looked up at the board and saw that Coach had written "Define Key Plays (Processes)." He turned back to look at them.

"What would you say are the key plays that keep your business running? Walk me through it," Coach prompted.

Ricki pictured herself as a customer, walking through the front doors of Accelerate Auto. She imagined a happy, smiling, uniformed employee behind the counter. Not Tori or Tessa. What was that girl's name? Oh, Tina. Yeah, not her.

"So the first step is the intake system or the check-in process. Customers come in, the store is clean and welcoming, a friendly employee welcomes them and offers to help."

Coach turned around to write that down and gestured with his hands for them to continue spitting out the key plays to run the shop.

"Then we do the diagnostics, figure out what's wrong with each vehicle," Anthony added.

"And then we follow up with the customer," said Ricki. "Let them know what the issue is, how we can fix it, how long we think it'll take, and a price estimate."

"Originally, we trained the team on two different ways to do this. There's one way to do a follow-up if the person leaves their car with us and another way to do it if they sit in the lobby and wait," Anthony continued.

Coach kept jotting down notes.

"So we get the approval from the customer, which gives the green light to the mechanic to start the service," Ricki said, squinting as she thought through each step.

"Alongside all of this, a key component is ordering inventory, stocking it, and keeping track of what we have and what we need," Anthony added.

"And we're also managing our relationship with a supplier to make sure we get the parts we need quickly."

Anthony and Ricki nodded at each other as Coach furiously wrote on the board. When they were quiet, he turned back around.

"Great. So does this look right?"

Coach used the marker to point to the board.

Define Key Plays (Process)

1. Intake system
2. Diagnostics
3. Follow-up with customers
4. Inventory
5. Supplier relationships

Ricki and Anthony nodded.

"So we've determined the key processes, or plays, that will help us win. Now what?"

Anthony thought back to his days on the field. "We practice them," he said confidently.

"Not yet. If there was a new guy on your team and he was in the locker room and your coach had written down the names of the plays up here, would he be able to go out and execute them right away?

"No," said Anthony. "He'd need to know what each one meant, how each one applied to him."

"And he'd do that by . . ."

"Asking questions?" Ricki offered.

Coach pointed his marker at her. "Bingo! You have to ask yourself questions about each of these plays so you can define them. Once they are defined and everyone knows what is expected of them, then you can practice. So, let's start at the top. What are some questions a new person would ask about how the intake system works? And how would you answer them? Those answers are going to be the clear, repeatable action steps that go into your playbook."

"So I guess some questions a new person would ask would be: How do I greet someone who enters the store, what information do I get from them, how do I input it into the system, and what do I do next?" Ricki said, putting up a finger as she listed each question out loud.

Coach wrote them down as she talked. "And how would you answer these questions?"

"When someone walks in, you smile, make eye contact, and welcome them to Accelerate. You ask what brings them in today, listen intently as they describe their problem, and input their information into the system," Anthony said. "Then you explain our process, ask them if they will be waiting in the lobby or dropping their car off, and check in with the mechanics to get an estimate for how long it will take to get a diagnostic." Ricki nodded in agreement.

"Okay, so let's write those down in the playbook. Let's break it down even further by expanding on each of those things. How do they put it into the system—what is the process for waiting versus dropping their car off?" Coach asked.

Ricki and Anthony opened the first page of their composition notebooks and started brainstorming. They turned their chairs together and started breaking down each play, clarifying the processes and taking time to define each step. Coach watched intently.

"Your goal should be to create a playbook that you can hand to a new employee and they will understand exactly what you expect and how to, step by step, walk through each play. Of course, you're not just going to hand them the playbook and walk away—that's where the practice comes in. But having this playbook on hand makes it so that everybody has the same vision and is running the same play."

"Oh," Ricki said, looking up from her notebook, "We also have to remember that we can get information via phone calls and emails. There has to be a whole different process and play for that." Coach nodded in agreement. "The answers you come up with form the structure of your system."

The group continued to brainstorm through the rest of the play. When they were finished, Ricki and Anthony had five or six pages in their notebooks filled, front and back, with key terms, step-by-step directions, and checklists.

"So that's one play," Coach said, and Ricki and Anthony looked up at him, surprised.

"And we do all of this," Ricki said, flipping through the pages, "for each of the plays."

"Yep. It's a lot of work. But so is winging it or putting bandaids on problems over and over again." Coach sat down at his desk and let Ricki and Anthony work through the remaining plays.

They discussed each step of the diagnostic process, who was responsible for running the diagnostic tests, what technology and systems they used, and how they documented their findings. Then they dove into how the follow-up process worked and created a systemized plan for those leaving their cars and another process for those waiting in the lobby. They discussed different ways to offer excellent customer service for those who would be waiting, including having sodas in a mini fridge, magazines and books to read, and even a small table and chairs with coloring books and crayons in the corner for kids. These new ideas led to even more questions, such as who would be responsible for stocking these things? Who would be in charge of keeping it all organized?

"It seems like each new idea comes with a whole different set of questions," Ricki noticed.

"That's exactly right, which is why your playbook is a living, breathing document. It's something that is steady and consistent, but can also be changed and updated as your business grows and expands," said Coach.

They moved on to the approval process and how to get verbal or written confirmation from the customer so that the repairs could start, and then how to make sure the mechanics had all of the information that they needed to do their jobs effectively.

"So then won't we need a whole playbook for just the service and repairs? So all the mechanics are out there using the same techniques and tools? And the repairs are done the same way every time?" Anthony asked, looking at Coach nervously.

"Yes, but that can wait. You'll probably want to sit down with the mechanics to get a better understanding of how they work and what their processes are. So for now, we stick to this," he said, leaning back in his chair and pointing to the whiteboard.

Ricki and Anthony moved on to managing inventory, and Coach noticed that this play caused quite a bit of confusion. Where they were able to seamlessly agree on the steps and processes for the other plays, here they came to a standstill.

"I thought Jodie checked inventory at our store once a week," Ricki said.

"I thought it was twice a week. And who does it at the other stores?" Anthony asked.

Coach listened as the couple quickly realized that they didn't have clarity when it came to inventory management. They discussed their conflicting assumptions about what triggered the system to flag for low inventory, and what the lead times were for reordering, and drew a blank when it came to who was responsible for final approval on new stock orders.

"Looks like this one is a bit messy," Anthony said apologetically, but Coach was all smiles. It reminded Ricki of his positive demeanor when she fell in the mud.

"That's okay! It's good! This is how our business tells us where it needs a little more attention. Not having the answers to this requires us to ask the questions, do the research, find the answers, and then implement them. Is there someone you could call to give you more clarity on this?" Coach asked.

Ricki pulled out her phone and called each store, asking them questions about how they handled inventory at each location. When she got off the phone, she looked defeated. "I got some answers, but it's clear that this is an area that needs a complete overhaul. Explains why a lot of our bad reviews are about parts not being available or service taking longer than quoted because we're waiting for parts," she sighed.

"You're putting the pieces together! This is where the magic happens!" Coach said excitedly. "Anthony, think of it like this. It's like if you played the whole game and then you didn't bother to review the stat sheet. You have to look at where you went wrong so you can improve for next time. That's what this is: reviewing the stat sheet."

Creating the play for inventory management took twice as long as the others, but they worked diligently to ask all of the right questions and stuck with it until they had a clear solution for each one. Once this was done, it was easier to tackle the final play: building and maintaining the relationships with the suppliers so that there was a fast turnaround time for items not in stock.

By the end of it, Ricki's hand was cramping from writing so much.

"Let's pause for lunch and come back to this in an hour," Coach suggested. "I'm starving." Everyone agreed and filed out of the office, and Anthony and Ricki hopped in the car and drove down to a local food truck park by the water, sharing a bread bowl of clam chowder and a giant lobster roll. They ate quietly, both lost in their own thoughts. Ricki pulled out the small composition notebook from her purse and flipped through it.

"I love this," she said, pointing to the book. "I love the idea of a playbook. We're athletes. Why didn't we think of this sooner?"

Anthony nodded with a mouth full of lobster. When he swallowed, he said, "I was thinking the same thing. I can't wait to bring this back to the team. It's going to help us get clarity on every aspect of our business." They finished their lunch, went back to the bed and breakfast, and met Coach back in his office.

"So we talked about creating a playbook, and that first we have to define the plays, and then we have to document them," said Coach. "Once you've got them defined and documented, then you . . ." He pointed to Anthony.

"Practice them?" he ventured.

"Bingo!" Coach said. "You have to commit to using your play-book for every aspect of your business. And I'll tell you right now, your first run is not going to be perfect. Your second or third probably won't be either. But that's okay. If you ran a play on the field and realized it wasn't going to work for whatever reason, you'd adjust the play. You'll do the same thing with your playbook."

"So it's kind of like reviewing the tape?" asked Anthony.

"Yes! You try it, then you look back at it and see what worked and what didn't. You get feedback from your team to see what they think and make the necessary adjustments. You don't beat yourself up because the play didn't work, you look at it as an opportunity to tweak it so that it does."

Coach let them sit in silence for a while, and then Ricki spoke up. "Having a playbook is going to allow us to work more efficiently and effectively. It's going to give us and our team so much more clarity and help us to work as a more coordinated unit instead of a bunch of free agents. We won't get it all right all the time, but I have a good feeling that this," she tapped the playbook, "will help us to prevent a lot of silly mistakes and give us more time and energy to focus on growth."

Coach smiled proudly, and Anthony put his hand on Ricki's leg and squeezed.

"I think we covered a lot today. You're going to walk away with a whole new perspective on what it means to systemize. Along with the other things we talked about this week . . ." Coach trailed off, gesturing for them to recall the fundamentals they'd learned throughout the week.

"Analyze," Ricki said, thinking back to the bike fiasco with a smile.

"Organize," Anthony added, picturing Nate and Clara's van.

"Strategize," Ricki said, more excitedly, thinking about the hike.

"Prioritize," Anthony said, smiling as an image of Captain Todd on the boat came to mind.

"And Systemize," Ricki finished.

Coach looked like a proud parent. "Amazing. Yes, with those five fundamentals, you can truly recalibrate to accelerate. I think you've made the most of your time here, and Edna and I are so excited to see how you take this information and go from surviving to thriving."

Anthony wasn't sure, but he thought he saw Coach's eyes tear up. The big man turned quickly to the whiteboard to erase it.

Ricki and Anthony spent the rest of the afternoon sitting next to each other on the porch swing, rotating between discussing what was in their playbooks and just sitting in contemplative silence. As the sun went down, Coach reappeared on the porch with a bag of marshmallows balancing on top of a box of graham crackers. He didn't have to say a word; Anthony and Ricki were soon on their feet and following him to the firepit.

When the s'mores were eaten and the fire was dying down, everyone cleaned up and headed back inside.

"I wish we didn't have to leave tomorrow," Ricki said as she climbed the porch steps. Edna put a small hand on her back and nodded. "Me either," she said softly, "but I am so glad you came. And I am so excited to see how you transform your business."

The house was quiet as everyone retreated to their rooms and fell asleep, exhausted after a busy and productive day.

You do not rise to the level of your goals. You fall to the level of your systems.

—James Clear, *Atomic Habits*

ACTION STEP

Create your first Business Playbook Process.

Identify One Core Process: Choose a critical area in your business (such as client onboarding, service delivery, or sales).

Map the Process: Use the Process Mapping Template, available at accelerateplaybook.com or by scanning the following QR code, to break down the process into clear, repeatable, step-by-step actions.

Assign Responsibility: Clearly document who is responsible for each step—every task must have an owner.

Document Tools & Systems: List the tools, software, or resources used at each step to ensure consistency and clarity.

Define Success Indicators: Establish simple KPIs or checkpoints to measure the process's effectiveness and spot issues early.

Review and Refine: Share your mapped process with your team, test it in real situations, and update as needed for continuous improvement.

Why this works: Systemizing your business creates predictable, high-quality outcomes, empowers your team, and gives you the freedom to focus on growth. Your first documented process becomes the foundation of a scalable "business playbook"—reducing chaos and making your business more resilient and less dependent on any one person.

CHAPTER 12

SUSTAINED MOMENTUM
Living the Accelerated Life

Early the next morning, Ricki and Anthony packed their bags before heading down for one final breakfast. Anthony noticed that Ricki's movements were slow and deliberate, where he felt like he was rushing around the room, trying to get everything done so they could get back home.

"You good, babe?" he asked, zipping up the suitcases.

She nodded. "Yeah, I just really loved our time here. I don't want to go." Ricki stared out the window.

Anthony walked over to her and wrapped her in a hug. "This was a great idea, and I'm so glad I listened to you when you said we needed time away. I'm sad to go too, but I'm on fire, on *fire*, babe, about what we can do with everything we learned when we get back. And we can always come back! This can be our yearly retreat," he said, pulling away from her and looking down into her eyes. She nodded again and took one last look at the Tulip Room before heading downstairs.

Edna had really outdone herself this time. Not only were blueberry pancakes stacked on plates in the middle of the table, but there was bacon, a big bowl of eggs, sliced fruit, hash browns, and an assortment of cereals laid out like a breakfast commercial.

"Can't let you leave on an empty stomach!" she chirped, pouring coffee into empty cups.

"She cooks like this when she's sad," Coach whispered with a smile. Anthony and Ricki sat down to eat, and when they were stuffed, Anthony grabbed their suitcases by the front door and they all moved out to the porch.

"I don't like goodbyes," Ricki said, fighting back tears.

"Me either," said Edna. "But it's not goodbye, it's—"

"See you next season!" Coach chimed in enthusiastically, holding out his hand for Anthony to shake. When Anthony put his hand in Coach's, Coach pulled him in for a tight hug. Ricki could hear Coach murmuring something to Anthony, but she couldn't quite make it out.

"Got your playbook?" Edna asked.

Ricki patted her purse. "Right here."

"And your one-page plan?" Edna asked again.

Ricki patted her purse again. "Right here."

"Good. Then you've got everything you need to get back there and thrive. I know you're going to do it. I can't wait to hear all about it." Edna wrapped Ricki in a tight hug of her own.

"I checked the traffic this time," Anthony said playfully, "and found a way we can go that won't have a lot of traffic. So we'll make it home in good time." Coach smiled a knowing smile and patted Anthony on the back.

When they couldn't avoid leaving anymore, Anthony grabbed their suitcases and put them in the trunk. He started the car, and they looked at Edna and Coach on the porch, him with his arm wrapped around her, and her with her head resting on his chest. Anthony honked, the couple waved, and they made their way down the driveway. Anthony looked back one more time to watch Edna and Coach disappear in his rearview mirror. As they approached the main road, Ricki glanced out her window.

"Huh. I didn't see that when we were driving in," she said, putting her finger to the window and pointing outside. A sign sat along the property line, partly covered by growing bushes. The wooden sign was hand-painted with the words "Welcome to The Off-Season" in white letters.

"I can't believe she let him name the bed and breakfast that," Ricki said with a smile, shaking her head.

"I think it's perfect," said Anthony. "The Off-Season. It's where you go to work on your business, not in your business. Coach and I talked about the importance of an off-season when we arrived. And if this place was anything, it was our off-season. Now we're stronger, faster, healthier, and more prepared to win moving forward.

And Coach knows that when people come here, when they truly take the time to invest in their off-season, they can go back into the game with a game plan that works."

Ricki put her hand on her husband's arm and smiled as he cruised down the highway, noticing something different about his posture. He looked like a new man: confident, capable, excited about the future. She didn't say anything about the climbing speedometer, knowing that driving fast was just a part of who he was. And it wasn't lost on her that on the way *to* the bed and breakfast, they'd moved at a snail's pace, due to their lack of planning. Now that they had a plan, it was smooth sailing back home, and Anthony could pick up his speed, roll down the window, and stick his hand out to feel the wind rushing over it.

They made it home with time to spare, and as they mounted the front porch, Anthony noticed something sitting by the front door. A gorgeous vase of yellow flowers, with a note sticking out. He picked up the note and read:

> *Hope you enjoyed the Tulip Room. And your time together. You two are a good team. Love you both.*
>
> *—Pen*

Anthony surprised himself by smiling instead of rolling his eyes and brought the vase to the kitchen table. They both sat down with their playbooks in front of them. "I can't wait to show this to the team," Anthony said, tapping the playbook.

"I was just going to say the same thing," Ricki said. "I think they are really going to appreciate this new system, and we're going to be better leaders for them. We're all going to feel more like a team and—"

A ding on her cell phone interrupted her. "It's the delivery confirmation for Mr. Brown's order. It got there," she said with a sigh of relief.

"That was fast!" Anthony said, and another ding came through on his phone.

"It's Mr. Brown. He said, 'Tires just got here. All good. Thanks for fixing this. Call you next month for the next order,'" Anthony read aloud in a robot voice, mimicking Mr. Brown's monotone voice.

"Well, coming from him, that's a rave review!" Ricki laughed.

"You know, I don't want to wait until tomorrow to go to the office. I think we should go . . ." Ricki started.

"Say less," Anthony said, then jumped up from the kitchen table, grabbed the car keys, and they were off to the office.

After Ricki and Anthony greeted everyone in the office, Anthony suggested they close up shop a little early and head back to Stu's.

"We're back with a new plan, and we can't wait to share it with you. Let's go back to Stu's, eat too much BBQ, and fill you guys in on some of the stuff we've learned," Anthony said as he waited for everyone to finish up their tasks and meet in the reception area. When the office was quiet and dark, the whole team filed out to the parking lot, Ricki and Anthony leading the way with a little pep in their step.

The smell of BBQ hit them as soon as they walked in the door. Then Ricki heard a familiar booming voice, and Stu came out from the kitchen and greeted the team. He wrapped Ricki in a firm hug, and she tried not to think about whether or not he was going to get BBQ sauce on her new blouse. As she hugged him, her eyes went instinctively to the picture of Stu and her dad behind the bar. A lifetime of memories washed over her, and she suddenly felt a wave of emotion. *He'd be proud*, Ricki thought to herself, and willed herself not to let tears well up in her eyes. But then her eyes shifted. Right next to the picture of her dad and Stu was a framed cross stitch, and Ricki gasped. She recognized the blue and red flowers around the border and the loopy script right away.

> *A dream written down with a date becomes a goal.*
>
> *A goal broken down into steps becomes a plan.*
>
> *A plan backed by action makes your dreams come true.*[*]

"Where did you get that?" Ricki asked, pointing to the picture frame. Stu released her and followed her finger to the far wall.

"Oh, that's been there! It's something your dad gave to me that weekend he made me close."

Ricki looked at him, confused.

"He never told you?" Stu asked. Ricki shook her head.

"Years ago, your dad made me close the restaurant for a weekend. *A whole weekend!* The busiest time for me. I thought he was crazy, but he insisted. That weekend we closed the doors and sat

---

[*] This saying is largely attributed to the writer Greg Reid.

right there." He pointed to a small booth in the back. "And we made a plan. He helped me change the way I was handling finances, we made systems for inventory, and we talked about building a great team." Stu looked at the small booth like he could still see his old friend there.

"That weekend, that time to stop and create a new plan, is what saved this place," Stu continued. "That's why we're still here. Your dad always used to get on me about that. I would be back in that kitchen making sauces and trying new recipes until I almost fainted from exhaustion. He told me I could work hard *and* sit back and give myself time and space to think and plan." Stu laughed. *Recalibrate,* Ricki thought.

"All this to say, I'm glad you prioritized stepping away, really thinking about what you need, and making a plan," Stu concluded.

A ding from the kitchen caught his attention, and he patted Ricki on the shoulder and disappeared behind the swinging kitchen doors. Ricki stood still for a moment. She hadn't known that part about her dad, but she was so grateful for that story now. She felt a sense of pride that she was on the right track and that stopping to recalibrate really was the best decision she could have made for her business and her marriage.

"Ready, Ricki?" Anthony asked, and she noticed the whole table was already seated and looking at her expectantly. She smiled, pulled the playbook out of her purse, and said:

"This is going to change everything."

EPILOGUE
A Year Later

Anthony kissed Ricki on the top of the head, grabbed his coffee mug, and looked around the kitchen for the keys.

"I'm starting the day at the Robinson location," he explained, grabbing the keys off the table, "and then I'll meet you back at the office."

Three months ago, Ricki and Anthony bought a small, empty auto parts store on Robinson Street and transformed it into their fourth location in the city. They had hired an excellent team, and held a successful grand opening where they met the people of the community and introduced them to their business. The expansion had been a dream for years, but it finally became reality thanks to the systems they'd put in place to streamline operations and free up their time to focus on growth.

"Sounds good. Just make sure you stop by the distributor today to check on that backorder we flagged last week," Ricki said.

"Already in my calendar," Anthony said with a wink. "And don't forget to finalize the new inventory workflow with Crystal." He was out the door. As soon as the door closed it opened again, and Anthony's head popped back through the door. "Oh, and this came for you," he said, tossing an envelope on the coffee table and shutting the door again. Ricki picked up the envelope and opened it.

> *Anthony and Ricki,*
>
> *Congrats on your new store! We are so proud of you. David and Darla texted us and said that next month they are coming back to Martha's Vineyard. We'd love to invite you two back to the bed and breakfast for a little reunion! We're hosting a community picnic on the property and inviting previous guests and important people from the community, and we'd love to see you! Please let us know if you can make it. Details below.*
>
> *—Coach and Edna*

Ricki took a picture of the letter and sent it to Anthony. Three dots popped up on the screen, and then his response: *Oh, we're going.*

Four weeks later, Anthony and Ricki drove up the familiar gravel driveway and both gasped when the familiar Victorian came into the place. Part of the backyard had been converted to a parking area where Trixie, decked head to toe in neon orange, was directing parking. Balloons were strung up from trees, there was music playing, and people were eating, mingling, and touring the bed and breakfast. There were food trucks lined up on one side of the yard, children playing games on the porch, and picnic tables draped in checkered tablecloths. Edna saw them from the porch and came quickly down the steps to greet them. Coach followed closely behind.

"We're so glad you're here! Come in, come in!" Edna said with a big smile. As they approached the porch, they saw David and Darla sitting in the rocking chairs, and the four exchanged hugs and handshakes.

Coach, David, and Anthony moved slowly to the far side of the porch, talking and catching up while Ricki looked around the yard.

"Wait. Is that . . . ?" she asked, squinting toward the food trucks. She bolted down the stairs, straight toward the bright yellow and teal food truck with *Recalibrate Coffee* written in chunky script on the side.

Clara leaned out the window and handed a customer a steaming cup of coffee, and her face lit up when her eyes locked with Ricki's.

"You did it!" Ricki said, jumping up and down. Clara squealed and came out from behind the coffee truck and gave Ricki a hug.

"It's been amazing! We came back a few months after our initial visit, and Coach and Edna told us all about the magic of having a playbook. We've used it religiously, and . . . look!" she said, pointing to the truck.

"I see! That's amazing! I can't wait to hear all about it! But go, you've got people waiting!" Ricki said and playfully pushed Clara back toward the truck.

Edna and Ricki stood in the middle of the yard for a bit in silence until Ricki turned to Edna and said a quiet, "Thank you." Edna just nodded and squeezed Ricki's hand.

The men rejoined them with plates of lobster rolls, sandwiches, and cups of ice cream, and they caught each other up on their lives. Travels, booming businesses, growing families—it was good news all around.

When the event died down and the parking lot emptied out, the couples sat quietly on the porch, a reflective energy washing over them.

"We're so glad you guys could come back," Coach said. "Let's do this every year." Everyone nodded in agreement, and the porch buzzed again with plans and conversation.

"The event was a success!" Darla commented, rocking back and forth in her chair. "What a good turnout!"

"It was," Edna agreed, "but I'm exhausted!"

"What do you say we head out to the firepit—for old times' sake?" Coach asked, standing up. Everyone followed and found their original spots in the colorful Adirondack chairs that surrounded the updated firepit.

Coach made sure everyone had a drink in his or her hand before he stood up to make a toast. He raised his glass and looked around the circle, his eyes lingering on each person.

"To friends who've become family," he began, his voice steady and heartfelt. "To dreams that started as quiet conversations on that porch and have since turned into realities we couldn't have imagined. To the lessons we've learned, the mistakes we've turned into stepping stones, and the systems we've built to carry us forward."

He paused, his smile widening. "And most of all, to the power of reflection and growth. No matter where the road takes us, may we always have the courage to pause with a purpose and adjust so we can develop the tools to accelerate."

Everyone raised their glasses and echoed, "To accelerate," and took a sip, the clink of glasses mingling with the crackle of the fire.

ACTION STEP

Download and fill out the "Acceleration Readiness Checklist" by scanning the following QR code or visiting accelerate playbook.com. This one-page self-assessment ensures your business is truly ready to scale by confirming you have:

- A clear, written plan (your one-page plan)
- A focused revenue strategy map
- Documented core systems and processes
- An aligned, empowered team around your company playbook
- A clear, ambitious goal to pursue next

How to Use the Checklist: Review each section and honestly assess your readiness. Identify any gaps or areas needing attention before accelerating growth. Set clear next steps for each area, ensuring your business is built for sustainable, scalable success. Share your completed checklist with your leadership team or advisor for feedback and accountability.

ACKNOWLEDGMENTS

Writing *Accelerate* has been a journey fueled by partnership, wisdom, faith, and unwavering support. We are grateful for every person who has poured into us and helped bring this vision to life.

To **Daniel Grissom**—thank you for your partnership, your insight, and your belief in our work. You have been a steady voice of excellence as we shaped the concepts behind this book.

To my father, **Albert Mayo**—you have been teaching business principles to me my entire life, not only through your words but through your discipline, consistency, and example. Thank you for laying the foundation that made this book possible.

To **Diana**—thank you for being such an important part of our team. Your effort, creativity, and dedication continue to push our ideas forward and elevate everything we build.

To **Apostles Billy and Cynthia Thompson**—your love, support, and encouragement have carried us through season after season. Thank you for helping us grow on our faith walk and reminding us of God's hand in our journey.

To **Pastor Todd**—thank you for believing in our vision, standing with us, and supporting our mission and message. Your leadership has been a blessing in more ways than you can imagine.

To **Peter and Tatiana Cancro**—thank you for allowing us to witness business success principles up close. Your openness and generosity have shaped our thinking and strengthened our business philosophy. We love you deeply.

To **Kane Minkus**—thank you for your wisdom, perspective, and strategic insight. Your guidance helped refine this project in powerful ways, and your influence is reflected throughout these pages.

To our adult children—**Wesley, Kendall, and Cori**—thank you for adding value to our lives and for always telling us the truth, even when it stretched us. You continue to inspire us, challenge us, and remind us why legacy matters. We hope our journey of entrepreneurship leaves a lasting impact on you and that the spirit of leadership, ownership, and possibility continues through each of you.

To all of you—your impact is woven into the heart of this work. Thank you for being part of our story, our growth, and our mission to help others accelerate in life and business.

We love you all.

NOTES

1. Christine Caine (@ChristineCaine), "Sometimes when you're in a dark place you think you've been buried, but you've actually been planted," Twitter (X), August 13, 2023, https://x.com/ChristineCaine/status/1690752319275905024.
2. "Promoting Innovation," US Department of State archived content, accessed July 29, 2025, https://2009-2017.state.gov/s/dmr/qddr/240919.htm.
3. Michael E. Porter, "What Is Strategy?" *Harvard Business Review* (1996), accessed July 29, 2025, https://hbr.org/1996/11/what-is-strategy.

ABOUT THE AUTHORS

WALTER BOND

Former NBA Player | Business Advisor | Peak Performance Speaker

Walter Bond always knew his biggest wins would come after basketball. Though he made it to the NBA as an undrafted underdog—playing for the Dallas Mavericks, Utah Jazz, and Detroit Pistons—he saw entrepreneurship as his true championship arena.

Today, Walter is a Hall of Fame speaker, best-selling author, and cofounder of **Peak Performers Huddle**, where he partners with his wife, Antoinette Bond, to help leaders, teams, and entrepreneurs recalibrate, elevate, and perform at the highest level—on purpose.

Walter's story is one of relentless belief and unstoppable momentum. He transformed rejection into opportunity, hustle into mastery, and now teaches others how to do the same. His signature *Shark Mindset*—inspired by his best-selling book *Swim!*—has become a global movement, empowering audiences to move forward with focus, discipline, and drive.

From boardrooms to arenas, Walter delivers more than motivation—he delivers blueprints. His keynotes, coaching programs, and books (*Swim!*, *Cultivate*, and *Accelerate*) are trusted by Fortune 500 companies, fast-growing startups, and mission-driven entrepreneurs alike.

Whether he's speaking to thousands or coaching one-on-one, Walter brings fire, clarity, and game-ready strategies. His passion is simple: helping people unlock what's already inside them—and teaching them how to win, again and again.

Walter Bond didn't just play the game—he mastered the mindset. Now, he's showing the world how to do the same.

ANTOINETTE BOND
Fourth-Generation Entrepreneur |
Business Strategist | Peak Performance Coach

Entrepreneurship is woven into Antoinette Bond's DNA. As a fourth-generation entrepreneur, she grew up witnessing the power of partnership and perseverance—first on her grandparents' farm, then in her parents' real estate development business in Miami. From an early age, she learned that vision, grit, and sacrifice could turn side hustles into family legacies. Her story is the American Dream—lived, led, and now taught.

Today, Antoinette is the cofounder and CEO of **Peak Performers Huddle**, a world-class training and development company she built with her husband, Hall of Fame speaker and former NBA athlete Walter Bond. Together, they coach entrepreneurs, executives, and teams to recalibrate, accelerate, and reach peak performance in business and life.

A certified business coach, author, and sought-after strategist, Antoinette is known for her no-fluff, high-impact approach. She is the co-author of *Cultivate* and *Accelerate*, powerful business playbooks that turn inspiration into systems for growth.

Her coaching style blends deep insight with real-world execution—guiding clients to create scalable success around their passion. She has helped countless professionals shift from burnout to breakthrough by mastering mindset, strategy, and systems.

Whether she's leading workshops, delivering keynotes, or coaching one-on-one, Antoinette brings clarity, confidence, and contagious belief that *you can do this*—because she's lived it, built it, and helped others do the same.